# Word Problems

## BY
## REBECCA DYE, D.A., and CAROL DYE-KELLER

COPYRIGHT © 1999 Mark Twain Media, Inc.

ISBN 1–58037–099–3

Printing No. CD–1329

Mark Twain Media, Inc., Publishers
Distributed by Carson-Dellosa Publishing Company, Inc.

# Table of Contents

Introduction to the Teacher .................................................................................. iv
Introduction to the Student .................................................................................. 1
    To Begin (Classroom Poster or Handout) ...................................................... 2

STEP ONE: READ THE RECIPE AND CHECK THE INGREDIENTS .................... 3
    (Break Down Skills)
    What's Not Needed? ...................................................................................... 4
        Exercise 1.1 ............................................................................................ 4
        Exercise 1.2 ............................................................................................ 5
    What Is Still Needed? .................................................................................... 6
        Exercise 1.3 ............................................................................................ 6
        Exercise 1.4 ............................................................................................ 7
    Draw Pictures to Illustrate ............................................................................ 8
        Exercise 1.5 ............................................................................................ 8
        Exercise 1.6 ............................................................................................ 9
        Exercise 1.7 ............................................................................................ 10
        Exercise 1.8 ............................................................................................ 11
        Exercise 1.9 ............................................................................................ 12
        Exercise 1.10 .......................................................................................... 13
    Make Charts to Solve .................................................................................... 14
        Exercise 1.11 .......................................................................................... 14
        Exercise 1.12 .......................................................................................... 15
        Exercise 1.13 .......................................................................................... 16
        Exercise 1.14 .......................................................................................... 17
        Exercise 1.15 .......................................................................................... 18
    Venn Diagrams .............................................................................................. 19
        Exercise 1.16 .......................................................................................... 19
        Exercise 1.17 .......................................................................................... 20
        Exercise 1.18 .......................................................................................... 21
    Sort, Organize, and Put Into Order ............................................................... 22
        Exercise 1.19 .......................................................................................... 22
        Exercise 1.20 .......................................................................................... 23
        Exercise 1.21 .......................................................................................... 24
        Exercise 1.22 .......................................................................................... 25
        Exercise 1.23 .......................................................................................... 26

STEP TWO: MIXING ........................................................................................... 27
    (Break Down Skills)
    Key Phrases: Addition ................................................................................... 28
        Exercise 2.1 ............................................................................................ 28
        Exercise 2.2 ............................................................................................ 29
        Exercise 2.3 ............................................................................................ 30

Key Phrases: Subtraction ........................................................... 31
    Exercise 2.4 ........................................................................ 31
    Exercise 2.5 ........................................................................ 32
    Exercise 2.6 ........................................................................ 33
More Than and Less Than ........................................................ 34
    Exercise 2.7 ........................................................................ 35
    Exercise 2.8 ........................................................................ 36
Key Phrases: Multiplication ....................................................... 37
    Exercise 2.9 ........................................................................ 37
    Exercise 2.10 ...................................................................... 38
Key Phrases: Division .............................................................. 39
    Exercise 2.11 ...................................................................... 39
    Exercise 2.12 ...................................................................... 40
    Exercise 2.13 ...................................................................... 41
Key Phrases: Addition, Subtraction, Multiplication, Division ............... 42
    Exercise 2.14 ...................................................................... 42
    Exercise 2.15 ...................................................................... 43
    Exercise 2.16 ...................................................................... 44
Name the Needed Operations .................................................... 45
    Exercise 2.17 ...................................................................... 45
    Exercise 2.18 ...................................................................... 46
    Exercise 2.19 ...................................................................... 47
    Exercise 2.20 ...................................................................... 48
    Exercise 2.21 ...................................................................... 49
    Exercise 2.22 ...................................................................... 50
    Exercise 2.23 ...................................................................... 51

STEP THREE: COOKING ........................................................... 52
(Full Problems)
Exercise 3.1: Order of Operations .............................................. 53
Exercise 3.2: Calendar and Time ............................................... 54
Exercise 3.3: Sports Store Sale ................................................. 55
Exercise 3.4: Town Track Meet .................................................. 56
Exercise 3.5: Combo Meals ...................................................... 57
Exercise 3.6: Clocks and Time ................................................... 58
Exercise 3.7: Graph Reading ..................................................... 59
Exercise 3.8: The Bakery ......................................................... 60
Exercise 3.9: Cookie Recipe ...................................................... 61
Exercise 3.10: School Supplies .................................................. 62
Exercise 3.11: School Supplies .................................................. 63
Exercise 3.12: The Kidz Store .................................................... 64
Exercise 3.13: The Kidz Store .................................................... 65
Exercise 3.14: Middle School Lunch ............................................ 66
Exercise 3.15: Middle School Lunch ............................................ 67
Exercise 3.16: Church Youth Trip ............................................... 68

Exercise 3.17: Sugar Cookies ............................................................... 69
Exercise 3.18: Spice Tea ..................................................................... 70
Exercise 3.19: Junk Food ..................................................................... 71
Exercise 3.20: Grocery Store ............................................................... 72
Exercise 3.21: Calories ........................................................................ 73
Exercise 3.22: Making Change ............................................................. 74
Exercise 3.23: Making Change ............................................................. 75
Exercise 3.24: Landscaping .................................................................. 76

STEP FOUR: TASTING ............................................................................ 77
(Break Down Skills)
Multiple Choice Estimation ................................................................. 78
 Exercise 4.1 ............................................................................... 78
 Exercise 4.2 ............................................................................... 79
 Exercise 4.3 ............................................................................... 80
 Exercise 4.4 ............................................................................... 81
Is the Amount Reasonable? ............................................................... 82
 Exercise 4.5 ............................................................................... 82
 Exercise 4.6 ............................................................................... 83
 Exercise 4.7 ............................................................................... 84
Estimation Practice: Rounding ........................................................... 85
 Exercise 4.8 ............................................................................... 85
Estimation Practice: Rounding and Solving Problems ....................... 86
 Exercise 4.9 ............................................................................... 86

ANSWER KEYS ...................................................................................... 87

# Introduction to the Teacher

Word problems have always been a source of anxiety for most students. Most of us remember having our parents and even our teachers frequently discuss their dislike of those dreaded "story problems." This text was written to break down the solving process into smaller components. It is often helpful to "digest" smaller amounts of material and work toward an answer, rather than to instantly attempt to come up with the final solution.

This text was written to be used as a supplement to a student's daily assignment or to provide additional practice in the area of word problems.

# Introduction to the Student

Doing math always makes me hungry. Maybe that's because I always completed my math homework at the kitchen table. Or maybe that's because I always did my math homework immediately after I came home and I was always hungry. Either way, I tend to put food and math together.

Think about your favorite snacks. Do you like candy bars? Is your favorite candy bar plain chocoloate, or does it have nuts? Is it full of caramel? Does it ooze with crispy crunchies or maybe peanut butter? Do you love bananas? Do you like chips? Do you just love popcorn? What about celery sticks, carrots, raisins, or even pizza? Did you ever notice that eating your favorite snacks and solving word problems have something in common? What do you think they might have in common?

What happens if you stuff too much of your favorite snack into your mouth at one time? I'll tell you what happens! You can't swallow. You can't chew. You can't breathe! You choke. You might cough and sputter. You might turn red. You might even end up with your best friend wearing your snack. (Thank you so much for that!)

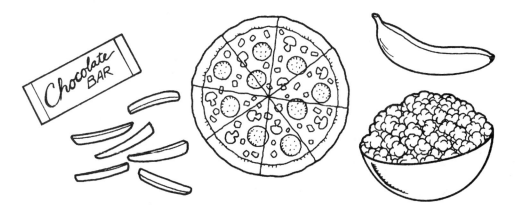

But of course, you don't have to eat that way. You have learned that to really enjoy your favorite snacks best, you enjoy them one bite at a time.

Solving word problems can be just like enjoying your favorite snack. To "finish off" the problem and NOT CHOKE, you need to take "one bite at a time."

Are you getting hungry, yet?

1

# TO BEGIN . . .

(Wash your hands and roll up your sleeves!)

When cooking a word problem, you can expect to do four main tasks:

## 1) Reading the recipe and checking the ingredients.
*Read the problem.
*Get the facts.

## 2) Mixing.
*Choose which operation (addition, subtraction, multiplication, division) applies.
*Write the equation.

## 3) Cooking.
*Solve the problem.

## 4) Tasting.
*Does the answer make sense?
*Is the answer correct?

# Step One: Read the Recipe and Check the Ingredients

Do you have what it takes? If you decided to bake some cookies, what would you do first? You would take the recipe and read it. Then you would check the cupboards to see if you had everything that the recipe required.

When starting a word problem, you must see if you have all the facts and understand what you need.

### 1. Read the recipe.

Read the problem. Take your time. This is NOT a race.

### 2. Check the pantry.

Illustrate what you have. Sometimes drawing a picture is helpful. You might also try using a graph, a chart, a table, or a sketch to help you visualize the problem.

### 3. Decide what you need or do not need.

Know what you're being asked to do. Decide if you have all the facts you need to complete the problem. Is there anything missing that you might really need to know? Did you include anything that is NOT needed?

Name _____     Date _____

**Exercise 1.1**

In each of the following, what information is NOT needed?

1. For breakfast, the triplets polished off two 8-ounce glasses of orange juice, four eggs, eight strips of bacon, six slices of toast, and one 6-ounce glass of grape juice. How many ounces did they drink?

_____

_____

2. In three days, Sue ate 17 chocolate chip cookies. Jane ate 12 cookies. Bob ate eight cookies, and Mom ate four cookies. How many more cookies did Sue eat than Bob?

_____

_____

3. Of the 427 potato chips in the bag, Jana ate 20 chips in five minutes. Jarret ate 15 chips in three minutes. How many chips did they eat?

_____

_____

4. John baked two dozen blueberry muffins. Jenny made three times as many sugar cookies, and Karin made six slices of cinnamon toast. How many cookies did Jenny make?

_____

_____

5. Phil ate 12 squares of pizza. Seven squares were pepperoni. Three squares were ham. Two squares were sausage. How many more squares of pepperoni than sausage did Phil eat?

_____

_____

6. Heather and Chad shared three boxes of popcorn at the movie. Nathan ate one soft pretzel and drank one 12-ounce orange soda. Bob drank two 10-ounce colas after eating two boxes of popcorn all by himself. How much soda was consumed?

_____

_____

Name _____    Date _____

**Exercise 1.2**

In each of the following, what information is NOT needed?

1. Abby gets paid $20 a week for running errands for her five neighbors. Three neighbors pay cash. Two neighbors pay every week. Two neighbors pay by check. Two neighbors pay once a month, and one neighbor pays every other week. How many neighbors still owe her money after two weeks?

_____

_____

2. Reread problem #1. How much does each neighbor pay?

_____

_____

3. Paul has 75 tickets to sell at $3.50 each. He has sold $\frac{2}{3}$ of the tickets. How many tickets has he sold?

_____

_____

4. Each of three friends has a 10-speed, a 15-speed, and an 18-speed bike. The first travels two miles at an average of 10 mph. The second travels $2\frac{1}{2}$ miles at an average speed of 12 mph. The last travels $3\frac{1}{2}$ miles at an average speed of 15 mph. How many miles (total) have they biked?

_____

_____

5. At the store, there were oranges at 40 cents each, apples at 30 cents each, and bananas at 25 cents each. How much would four apples and seven bananas cost?

_____

_____

6. A teacher has taught third grade for six years. She had 14 girls and 12 boys for three years in a row. The other three years she has had 16 girls and 14 boys. How many girls has she had in her six years of teaching?

_____

_____

Name _____ Date _____

**Exercise 1.3**

Tell what information (if any) has been left out and is still needed to complete these problems.

1. Mrs. Kitchen has a large box of felt sheets. There are 32 students in her class. How many pieces of felt does each student get?

_____

_____

2. Mr. Tank can spend $50 on lunches for his 20 students on the field trip. Can he buy each of them a meal costing $2.30?

_____

_____

3. Abby gets paid $20 a week running errands for five different neighbors. Three neighbors pay cash. Two pay every week. Two pay by check. Two pay once a month, and one pays every other week. How much does each pay?

_____

_____

4. Jacob went shopping with $35. He bought a $15 pair of shorts, a $10 T-shirt, a package of socks, and an ice cream cone costing $1.25. How much does he still have left?

_____

_____

5. A group of friends worked together to mow a churchyard and cemetery. They earned $75. How much did each earn?

_____

_____

Name _____ Date _____

**Exercise 1.4**

Tell what information (if any) has been left out and is still needed to complete these problems.

1. Bryson's uncle has 12 players on his baseball team. He has $300 to spend on equipment and soda for the players. How much is left to spend on soda for the players?

_____

_____

2. Cameo is treasurer for his class of 28 students. He has collected $150 from class members for pictures. Have all the members paid for pictures?

_____

_____

3. Holly sent 15 invitations to her birthday party. Eight people said "yes" to the invitation. Four people cannot attend, and three people are not sure. Are at least half of the people Holly invited coming to the party?

_____

_____

4. Javan brings soda for refreshments after football camp. Will two cases (of 24 cans each) be enough?

_____

_____

5. The students in Mrs. Patterson's class are reading books to win free pizzas. Aiden has read four books with 70 pages in each book. How many more books does Aiden need to read in order to win a pizza?

_____

_____

Name _____  Date _____

**Exercise 1.5**

Drawing a picture is often a helpful way to illustrate a problem. Draw a picture, diagram, chart, or table to help you visualize each of these situations. You do not need to solve the problems. Some of these problems may be very simple. Others may be more involved. The idea here is to picture in your mind the situations being described.

1. Eight children wore mittens to school. Five of them wore blue mittens. Two wore green, and one wore red. Three other children wore boots. Two children wore black boots, and one wore blue boots. Seven other children wore hats. Three of them wore blue hats. Two of them wore red hats. One wore black, and one wore green. How many children were there in all? How many children wore blue items? How many wore red items?

2. The school cafeteria has rectangular tables that seat eight children when three sit at each side and one sits at each end. How many tables will it take to seat 30 children? How many tables will it take to seat 50 children when the tables are pushed together end-to-end?

3. You have a piece of paper the shape of an octagon (like a stop sign). You want to cut it into triangles. What is the smallest number of triangles (the fewest) into which you can divide the octagon? (The triangles do not need to be the same shape or size.)

    8

Name _____ Date _____

**Exercise 1.6**

Draw more pictures!

1. Mrs. Smith's class is going on a field trip. Three cars have room for four children each. Five children can ride in each of two vans, and three cars have room for three children each. Is there enough room for 27 children to go on the field trip?

2. Mrs. Smith's 27 students will be sitting in an auditorium to watch a film. There are two rows of six chairs, three rows of four chairs, and three rows of three chairs. Is there enough for all of them to sit down?

3. These same 27 students will do group reports and projects. One group of five can work together on a map. Three groups of four can report on the places they went. How many groups of two or three could work together on other reports so that all the children are members of a group? There may be more than one answer.

Name _____ Date _____

**Exercise 1.7**

Draw more pictures! (You do not need to solve the problems.)

1. Dan punched eight holes in a piece of paper and numbered the holes in order. The holes were equally spaced with three centimeters (cm) between the centers of the holes. How far is it from hole #2 to hole #6?

2. A covered walkway was built across the front of several downtown shops. This canopy was supported by 14 metal posts that were nine feet apart. How far is it between post #3 and post #11?

3. Chris put together his model train set. The engine was 14 centimeters (cm) long. Each of the seven boxcars was 11 cm long. There was one cm before and after each car and the engine. How long was the train?

4. Kurt plants flowers along the edge of his garden. He leaves a blank space of six inches at the beginning and at the end of each row, and he leaves six inches between each plant. He plants 20 different flowering plants. How long is the garden row?

5. An athlete runs the fire escape steps in a local building to train for the Olympics. He begins at ground level and runs to the middle floor. He then runs down three floors, turns around, and runs seven floors to the top. How many floors are in the building?

Name _____ Date _____

**Exercise 1.8**

Draw more pictures. Do not solve the problems.

1. Abe flew three kites. One kite flew 400 feet in the air. Another flew $\frac{1}{2}$ that height, and another flew $\frac{1}{5}$ of 400 feet. How high did each kite fly?

2. Four friends mowed yards. Together, they made $70 by charging the same amount for each yard. Bill mowed two lawns. Mark mowed one yard. Keith mowed twice as many as Bill, and Joe mowed as many as Bill and Mark together. How many yards did they mow? How much did they earn on each lawn?

3. A telephone pole is 30 feet tall. The shadow of the pole on the ground is 40 feet long. How far is it from the top of the pole to the end of the shadow?

4. Ann has blue jeans, black jeans, and black wind pants. She also has four T-shirts that can be worn with all three pairs of pants. How many different outfits can she wear?

Name_____ Date _____

**Exercise 1.9**

Draw a picture or diagram to illustrate and solve each situation.

Mr. and Mrs. Brown were married 40 years ago. On their first Christmas, they gave each other one gift, which meant that two total gifts were exchanged. Years passed, and they eventually had three children.

1. The Brown family is comprised of Mr. and Mrs. Brown and their three children. If each of the five people gave each and every other person exactly one gift, how many total gifts would be exchanged at Christmas?

2. Several years later, their family had grown to 10 people. If each of these people gave each and every other person exactly one gift, how many total gifts would be exchanged?

Name_____ Date _____

**Exercise 1.10**

Draw a picture/diagram to illustrate and solve each situation.

1. At a local deli, Joe decides to order a submarine sandwich. He can choose from wheat or white bread, and there are three different meat combination choices. He then can choose from lettuce, tomato, and cheese—either none, one, two, or all three. How many sandwich combinations are possible?

2. At the same deli, Joe can order ice cream sundaes. He may choose one flavor from chocolate, vanilla, or strawberry ice cream. There are also three topping flavors from which he may choose one or more or none. He may then decide if he wants whipped cream, nuts, both whipped cream and nuts, or neither. How many combinations are possible?

Name_____ Date _____

**Exercise 1.11**

Sometimes a chart can be helpful to plan or eliminate answers. Use the chart to help you put the information together. Then, make your own chart to do the next problem.

1. There are four cans of soda in the refrigerator: one orange, one grape, one lemon-lime, and one cola. Chart which soda each will choose.

   A. Janna and John do NOT like grape.
   B. Janna and Jenny are allergic to cola.
   C. Janna and Jenny do NOT like anything with lemon.
   D. Jarret prefers soda that does not have a fruit flavor.
   E. Jenny and John do NOT like orange.

| | Orange | Grape | Lemon-lime | Cola |
|---|---|---|---|---|
| Jenny | | | | |
| John | | | | |
| Janna | | | | |
| Jarret | | | | |

2. The same four children need to clean house. Chart what each will choose to do.

   A. Neither John nor Jarret likes to dust or vacuum.
   B. Janna prefers to dust or clean sinks.
   C. Jarret prefers cleaning sinks rather than gathering trash from the wastebaskets.

Name_____ Date _____

**Exercise 1.12**

Make charts to complete the following situations.

1. Ann, Sue, Joy, and Dot competed in the same event in a tumbling meet. Ribbons were awarded for the first, second, third, and fourth place winners.

   A. Not all of the girls received ribbons.
   B. Ann and Joy won ribbons for placing neither first nor fourth place.
   C. Of the four girls, Joy placed the lowest of those getting ribbons.
   D. Dot did the best of all the girls, and Ann did not get third place.

2. The same four girls all competed in at least one of the four other events at the tumbling meet, for a possible total of five events each.

   A. Ann competed in all of the events.
   B. Sue competed in half as many events as Dot.
   C. Dot competed in one less event than Ann.
   D. No one competed in the same number of events.

15

Name _____ Date _____

**Exercise 1.13**

Make charts to complete the following situations.

1. There are six weight lifting stations through which Al, Bob, Carl, Dale, Evan, and George will circulate. The stations are the bench press, the military press, squats, curls, lateral pull downs, and toe raises. Each of the six weight lifters will begin with one of his favorite stations.

   A. Al, Dale, and George don't like the military press, squats, or lateral pull downs.
   B. Bob does not like the military press or toe raises.
   C. Carl does not like squats, curls, or toe raises.
   D. Evan does not like squats or the military press.
   E. Al does not like the toe raises or the bench press, and Dale doesn't like the bench press.

2. The Green family is picking out which of the four sets of colored bed sheets to put on their children's beds. There is one set each of white, blue, green, and yellow sheets. Zane and Fred refuse to sleep on yellow sheets. Sally doesn't like green sheets. Rachel hates green and white sheets. Mom won't put white sheets in the boy's room, and Fred would rather not have blue sheets.

16

Name _____ Date _____

**Exercise 1.14**

Make charts to complete the following problems.

1. Sarah, Emily, Alwin, Rick, and Sharon decided which popsicle flavor each likes best. Emily, Sarah, and Alwin don't like lime or grape. Sarah and Sharon are allergic to cherry, and Rick and Emily are allergic to lime and blueberry. Alwin really doesn't like blueberry or orange.

2. Each of the same five people (Sarah, Emily, Alwin, Rick, and Sharon) cleans his or her own room once a week. They decided that each of them will be responsible for cleaning one extra room each week. The extra rooms each will be responsible for cleaning could be the living room, kitchen, hall bathroom, guest bedroom, and office. Emily is too short to make beds. Rick and Sharon prefer to clean the kitchen or the office. Sarah really dislikes cleaning sinks or counter tops. Alwin and Rick always do a good job remembering to vacuum upholstered chairs in the office or the living room.

Name _____ Date _____

**Exercise 1.15**

Use the following clues and chart to answer the question.

Nine friends play different positions on a softball team. What position does each play?

| Claire | Tracy | Janna | Kari |
|--------|-------|-------|------|
| | Michelle | Elaine | Whitney |
| | Jenny | Rachel | |

1. The coach does not want Claire, Jenny, Rachel, Whitney, Kari, and Janna to play in the outfield.

2. Janna, Rachel, Tracy, Michelle, and Kari don't pitch or catch.

3. Whitney, Jenny, Michelle, and Janna don't like to play at 1st, 2nd, or 3rd base.

4. Whitney prefers pitching or playing short stop.

5. Claire and Elaine prefer pitching, playing 2nd base, or playing right field.

6. Kari and Tracy prefer playing 1st base, left field, or short stop.

|          | Pitch | Catch | 1st | 2nd | 3rd | S.Stop | RF | LF | CF |
|----------|-------|-------|-----|-----|-----|--------|----|----|----|
| Claire   |       |       |     |     |     |        |    |    |    |
| Michelle |       |       |     |     |     |        |    |    |    |
| Tracy    |       |       |     |     |     |        |    |    |    |
| Jenny    |       |       |     |     |     |        |    |    |    |
| Elaine   |       |       |     |     |     |        |    |    |    |
| Janna    |       |       |     |     |     |        |    |    |    |
| Rachel   |       |       |     |     |     |        |    |    |    |
| Whitney  |       |       |     |     |     |        |    |    |    |
| Kari     |       |       |     |     |     |        |    |    |    |

Name _____ Date _____

**Exercise 1.16**

Use the Venn diagram to answer these questions.

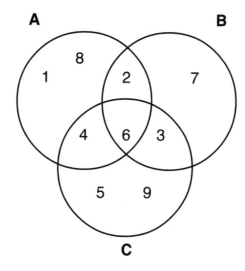

1. What number(s) are in both circles A and B?

_____

2. What number(s) are in circle B but not C?

_____

3. What number(s) are in B and C but not A?

_____

4. What number(s) are in A but not B?

_____

5. What number(s) are in A and B but not C?

_____

6. What number(s) are in A, B, and C?

_____

7. What number(s) are not in B but are in A and C?

_____

Name_____ Date _____

**Exercise 1.17**

Fill in the Venn diagram below to illustrate and answer the following.

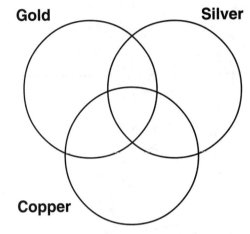

There are 25 collectors in the Mid America Coin Collector Club. Four collect only gold and silver coins. Five collect only gold coins. Two collect only silver and copper coins, and four collect only gold and copper coins. There are a total of 14 gold collectors and 10 silver collectors.

1. How many collect all three types of coins?

_____

2. How many collect only silver coins?

_____

3. How many collect only copper coins?

_____

4. How many collect any two types of coins?

_____

5. How many collect only one type of coin?

_____

Name_____ Date _____

**Exercise 1.18**

Draw Venn diagrams to illustrate each.

1. Mrs. High's class of 20 students went out for ice cream sundaes. Everyone chose hot fudge or strawberry topping. Two students had only hot fudge. Three had only strawberry. One student had both hot fudge and strawberry with no whipped cream. Four had both hot fudge and whipped cream and no strawberry. Four had strawberry with whipped cream and no hot fudge. How many had all three?

2. Achievement tests were given to 15 students in math, language arts, and science. No one took all three exams. Four students took only the math portion of the test. Two students took only the language arts portion. One took only the science portion of the test, and one took both the math and the science portions. A total of six students took the science test, and a total of nine students took the language test. How many took BOTH the science AND language tests?

Name_____   Date _____

**Exercise 1.19**

Sort, organize, and put the facts into order.

1. Mona had the highest batting average on her team. Wanda's average was higher than Beth's but was less than Carol's average. List how the girls ranked from the highest to the lowest.

   Highest average        _____

                          _____

                          _____

   Lowest average         _____


2. Andy had the least missed shots of all his friends. Ben had fewer than Will. Glen had fewer than Ben. Who had the most missed shots?

   Most missed shots  _____

                      _____

                      _____

   Least missed shots _____


3. Raymond led the race. Jay was ahead of Richard but was behind Mike. Dale was behind Richard and was ahead of Colin. Who came in last?

   First place            _____

                          _____

                          _____

                          _____

                          _____

   Last place             _____

Name_____ Date _____

**Exercise 1.20**

Sort, organize, and put the facts in order.

1. The Warriors won the conference championship two years in a row. The Eagles won it after the Warriors but before the Panthers won. The Tigers won it before the Warriors. Who was the last team to win the conference?

   The last team to win  _____

   _____

   _____

   The first team to win  _____

2. Bob's test score was higher than Tim's. Sue had the highest score. Ellen's score was lower than Tim's score. Who had the second and third highest scores?

   The highest score  _____

   _____

   _____

   The lowest score  _____

3. Kent has more baseball cards than anyone. Mary has more than Jade but fewer cards than Jack. Sam has the least cards of all. Who has the second most cards?

   The most cards  _____

   _____

   _____

   _____

   The least cards  _____

Name_____ Date _____

**Exercise 1.21**

Sort, organize, and put the facts in order.

1. The Renegades have a winning streak shorter than the Sharks. The Vikings have a winning streak longer than the Renegades. The Bears' winning streak is shorter than the Renegades. The Sharks' streak is longer than the Vikings' streak. Who has the longest and shortest streak?

   The longest streak _____

   _____

   _____

   The shortest streak _____

2. The Citizenship Award is given each year to an outstanding high school junior. Joe won it in 1993. Mike won it before Joe. Annette won it after Joe but before Barb won it. Who won it first?

   The first winner    _____

   _____

   _____

   The last winner    _____

3. Springfield gym is larger than Brownsville's gym but is smaller than the one in Davis City. The gym at Carlton is the largest of all. What is the smallest gym?

   The smallest gym    _____

   _____

   _____

   The largest gym    _____

Name_____ Date _____

**Exercise 1.22**

Sort, organize, and put the facts in order.

1. The Oak Hill snowfall total was higher than the Fulton total. The Maple total was less than the Twin Falls total. Fulton's total was more than the Twin Falls total, but the Twin Falls total was less than Oak Hill's total. Who had the largest and smallest amounts of snow?

   Largest      _____

                _____

                _____

   Smallest     _____


2. Armond, Stonee, Hayley, and Catlin have had the best attendance records of first, second, third, and fourth grades. Stonee has fewer absences than Hayley but more than Catlin. Armond has more than Hayley. Who had the most and the least absences?

   Most         _____

                _____

                _____

   Least        _____


3. Jamario had the lowest golf score of the tournament. Desiree's score was lower than Ivan's but was higher than Shelby's score. Marcus shot seven strokes higher than any of these players. List the five golfers from the lowest to the highest score.

   Lowest       _____

                _____

                _____

                _____

   Highest      _____

Name _____     Date _____

**Exercise 1.23**

Sort, organize, and put the facts in order.

1. Four communities decided to recycle aluminum cans. Lenox recycled more than Salem but recycled less than Belleview. Freeburg recycled less than Salem. What community came in first?

    First place     _____

    _____

    _____

    Fourth place     _____

2. Spencer, Antonio, Skylar, Terrance, Montel, and London all entered the hot dog eating contest at the county fair. Skylar ate more than Terrance but less than Antonio. Montel ate less than Terrance but more than London. Spencer ate more than Antonio. How did the six people place?

    First place     _____

    _____

    _____

    _____

    _____

    Sixth place     _____

3. Tyrus, Dante, Molly, and Kelsey all have regular dental check-ups. Dante had his check-up before Tyrus. Molly had hers before Dante. All three had their check-ups after Kelsey. Who had the most recent check-up?

    Most recent     _____

    _____

    _____

    _____

# Step Two: Mixing

Once you have the ingredients, you must know what to do with them. Mixing can involve one or a combination of operations. Putting ingredients together requires addition. Measuring ingredients might require addition as well as subtraction. Making a double recipe requires multiplication. Making half of a recipe requires some division. Which operation will you need to perform? Which must come first?

Look for clue words and phrases that suggest what to do with the facts. Will you be …

## Adding?

Look for phrases like "find the sum," "put together," or "find the total."

## Subtracting?

Look for phrases such as "find the difference," "compare," "take away," "how many more are needed," "how much was left," or "what remained."

## Multiplying?

Look for phrases like "find the product of" or "20 percent of."

## Dividing?

Look for phrases such as "how many equal groups or sets" or "find the quotient."

**CAUTION:** Some problems will ask you to do more than one operation.

### *Now, write the equation!*

Name_____  Date _____

**Exercise 2.1**

Key words or phrases that imply (hint) that addition is needed include:

Find the sum …
Put together …
Find the total …
Combine …
Add …

Write the mathematical expression for each of these and solve them.

1. What is the total of 168, 947, and 89?

2. Put together the largest three numbers of 9, 19, 82, 93, 54, 28, and 87.

3. What is the total sum of 87.9, 6.73, and 4.08?

4. How much is $4.27, $16.28, $47.92, and $32.59?

5. Combine 8,746 and 96,487.

6. Find the sum of 8.9, 4.7, and 63.8.

Name_____ Date _____

**Exercise 2.2**

Write the mathematical expression for each and solve.

1. What is the total of 48,387; 3,580; and 259?

2. Combine the smallest four numbers among 87.4, 86.2, 39.2, 79.5, and 90.4.

3. Put 81.29, 64, and 0.47 together.

4. Add $16.47, $1.63, and $227.18.

5. Find the sum of $47.99, $52.12, $6.50, and $12.69.

6. How much is 15,320; 620; 547; and 12?

7. What is the total of 12.7, 63.9, 45, and 0.51?

Name_____ Date _____

**Exercise 2.3**

Write the mathematical expression for each and solve.

1. What is the total of $\frac{2}{5}$, $\frac{3}{4}$, and $\frac{1}{2}$?

2. Combine 0.14, 26.7, 6.032, and 28.

3. Put $\frac{4}{9}$, $\frac{2}{3}$, and $\frac{1}{4}$ together.

4. Total the three smallest numbers among 0.07, 0.28, 0.14, 0.007, and 0.014.

5. Total the three largest numbers among $\frac{1}{6}$, $\frac{2}{7}$, $\frac{2}{3}$, $\frac{1}{2}$, $\frac{3}{4}$, and $\frac{3}{5}$.

6. In all, how much is 75 cents, 97 cents, 55 cents, and 1 dollar and 23 cents?

Name_____ Date _____

**Exercise 2.4**

Key words or phrases that imply (hint) that subtraction is needed include:

How many more do you have …
How many more do you need …
What's the difference between …
What amount is still needed …
How many fewer are there …
How much less …
Subtract — from — …

Write the mathematical expression for each and solve.

1. What is the difference between 9,118 and 4,381?

2. How much more is 15,384 than 6,154?

3. How much less is 28 than 82?

4. Subtract 8.2 from 20.

5. How much more do you need to go from 39 to 78?

6. How many fewer is 486 than 673?

7. What amount is needed to go from $82.16 to $100.00?

Name_____ Date _____

**Exercise 2.5**

Write the mathematical expression for each and solve.

1. What is the difference between 826.4 and 59.63?

2. How much more is 68.05 than 4.0372?

3. How much less is 6.4 than 10.01?

4. Subtract 17.58 from 81.9.

5. How much more do you need to go from $6.29 to $10.00?

6. How much less is 0.001 than 0.01?

7. What amount is needed to go from $13.25 to $1,000.00?

Name _____ Date _____

**Exercise 2.6**

Write the mathematical expression for each and solve.

1. What is the difference between $\frac{7}{12}$ and $\frac{5}{16}$?

2. How much more is $\frac{25}{27}$ than $\frac{1}{4}$?

3. How much less is $\frac{3}{14}$ than $\frac{11}{13}$?

4. Subtract $\frac{3}{8}$ from $\frac{6}{7}$.

5. How much more do you need to go from $\frac{1}{7}$ to $\frac{8}{9}$?

6. What amount is needed to go from $\frac{5}{14}$ to $\frac{5}{6}$?

# MORE THAN and LESS THAN

The phrases MORE THAN and LESS THAN often create some problems for students. (Notice that the two words are not separated by other words or numbers and will have numbers on either side. Here are two examples: 7 more than 15; 6 less than 12.)

Most of us remember that MORE THAN requires addition and LESS THAN requires subtraction. The difficulty comes in the ORDER that the mathematical phrase is written. While order is not a problem in addition, it does create a huge problem with subtraction.

In general, when you see the phrase MORE THAN or LESS THAN coming in a mathematical expression, write the number from RIGHT to LEFT, not from left to right. (I know this sounds nutty, but trust me. This works!)

For example, if you are given the phrase 8 LESS THAN 14, you should:

1. Write the 8.                                                                           8
2. Realize that LESS THAN requires subtraction,
   but write it IN FRONT of the 8.                                                     - 8
3. Complete the expression by writing the 14.                              14 - 8

Try this with me.   17 LESS THAN 42 = ?
                              17
                            - 17
                        42 - 17

The same rule can be applied to MORE THAN even though order does not affect the resulting answer with addition. (Addition is communitive.)

For example: If you are given the phrase, 4 MORE THAN 15, you should:

1. Write the 4.                                                                           4
2. Realize MORE THAN requires addition,
   but write it in front of the 4.                                                      + 4
3. Complete the expression by writing the 15.                           15 + 4

Consistently writing MORE THAN and LESS THAN in this "backward" way will be helpful now and especially later when you use letters in place of numbers in mathematical expressions and equations.

Name_____ Date _____

**Exercise 2.7**

Use the "backward" way for MORE THAN and LESS THAN to write each phrase and then solve.

1. 52 more than 167

2. 6.8 less than 7.59

3. 864 less than 1,000

4. 9,642 more than 37

5. 2.5 less than 368

6. 48 more than 597

7. 163 more than 9,654

8. 13.14 less than 40.06

Name _____  Date _____

**Exercise 2.8**

Use the "backward" way for MORE THAN and LESS THAN to write each phrase and then solve.

1. $\frac{2}{3}$ more than $\frac{13}{14}$

2. $\frac{5}{8}$ more than $\frac{7}{6}$

3. $\frac{1}{4}$ less than $1\frac{2}{5}$

4. $\frac{1}{7}$ less than $\frac{8}{9}$

5. 0.07 more than 1.482

6. 0.14 less than 2.7

7. 0.49 less than 61

8. 3.01 more than 16.9

Name _____ Date _____

**Exercise 2.9**

The word OF in a mathematical expression usually indicates that we need to multiply. For example, taking $\frac{1}{2}$ of 30 means $\frac{1}{2}$ x 30, which is 15. Taking 40% of 20 means 0.40 x 20, which is 8.

Remember: When you change a percentage to a decimal, you move the decimal point two places to the left. Also, you do NOT need a common denominator when multiplying fractions!

Write each phrase as a mathematical expression. Ask your teacher if you are to go ahead and solve the problem.

1. 35% of 80

2. 40% of 60

3. 28% of 50

4. 30% of 90

5. 54% of 160

6. 76% of 300

7. $\frac{1}{3}$ of 63

8. $\frac{1}{5}$ of 75

9. $\frac{3}{4}$ of 60

10. $\frac{2}{7}$ of 77

11. $\frac{5}{6}$ of 48

12. $\frac{1}{8}$ of 56

Name _____  Date _____

**Exercise 2.10**

As we said earlier, the word OF often indicates that multiplication is needed. You may also see the phrase "find the product of ..." when multiplication is needed. Write the mathematical expression for each situation and solve it.

1. 8 groups of 25

2. the product of 39 and 16

3. 72 equal rows of 3 plants in each row

4. 14 groups of 12

5. the product of 21 and 3

6. 46 rows of chairs with 12 chairs in each row

7. 17 groups of 28

8. $\frac{2}{5}$ of a group of 30 pupils

9. the products of $\frac{1}{2}$ and $\frac{2}{3}$

10. $\frac{1}{4}$ of $\frac{5}{6}$

11. the product of $\frac{3}{4}$ and 62

12. $\frac{1}{2}$ of 56 cars

13. $8\frac{1}{2}$ rows of 6 houses in each row

14. $3\frac{1}{6}$ groups of 12

Name_____ Date _____

**Exercise 2.11**

　　　Dividing may be indicated by phrases such as "find the quotient" or "how many equal sets or groups are there in …" or simply the word *divide.*

Write the mathematical expression for each situation and solve these problems.

1. How many equal sets of 7 are there in 182?

2. Find the quotient of 672 and 16.

3. Divide 5,270 by 85.

4. How many equal groups are there if 356 is separated into groups of 4?

5. Find the quotient of 4,425 and 59.

6. Divide 16 by $\frac{6}{7}$.

7. How many equal groups of 3 are there in 9,672?

Name_____ Date _____

**Exercise 2.12**

Write the mathematical expression for each situation and solve these problems.

1. Divide 1,628 by 37.

2. Find the quotient of 2,660 and 28.

3. How many sets of 6 are there in 252?

4. Divide 1,005 by 15.

5. Find the quotient of 1,792 and 28.

6. How many equal groups of 7 are there in 343?

7. Find the quotient of 384 and 12.

Name _____ Date _____

**Exercise 2.13**

Write the mathematical expression for each and solve.

1. Divide 13.364 by 0.26.

2. Find the quotient of 27.48 and 6.

3. How many equal groups of 0.45 are there in 3.87?

4. You have 45.44 grams and share it equally with 8 students. How much does each student have?

5. Divide $\frac{4}{9}$ by $\frac{2}{7}$.

6. What is the quotient of $\frac{17}{80}$ and $\frac{1}{4}$?

7. How many equal groups of $\frac{4}{9}$ are there in 20?

Name _____ Date _____

**Exercise 2.14**

Write the mathematical expression for each and solve.

1. How many fewer is 87 than 200?

2. Combine $4.48, $13.56, and 76 cents.

3. How many equal groups of 4 are there in 27.2?

4. What is 18.9 more than 46.7?

5. What is 30% of 92?

6. Find the quotient of 54.027 and 8.7.

7. How much change will you receive if your total is $7.52 and you pay with a $10 bill?

8. What is the total of 8.7, 0.02, 96, and 0.254?

Name_____ Date _____

**Exercise 2.15**

Write the mathematical expression for each and solve.

1. What is 2.8 less than 82?

2. What is $\frac{1}{3}$ of 255?

3. Combine 879, 276, and 14,128.

4. Separate 343 into 7 equal groups.

5. What is 29% of 53?

6. What is the difference between 179.46 and 28.001?

7. What is the quotient of 3.268 and 0.43?

8. Put $\frac{2}{9}$, $\frac{1}{6}$, and $\frac{2}{3}$ together.

Name _____          Date _____

**Exercise 2.16**

Write the mathematical expression for each and solve.

1. Put together $\frac{2}{5}$, $\frac{1}{10}$, $\frac{7}{20}$, and $\frac{3}{4}$.

2. How many equal groups of 13 are there in 115.7?

3. What is 27% of 34?

4. What is the difference between $\frac{15}{16}$ and $\frac{2}{7}$?

5. What is the quotient of 274.50 and 18.3?

6. What is $\frac{2}{7}$ of 406?

7. Combine $\frac{2}{11}$, $\frac{1}{3}$, and $\frac{3}{4}$.

8. How much less is 14.963 than 36.7?

Name _____     Date _____

**Exercise 2.17**

Suppose that * represents any number. Tell what operation—addition (+), subtraction (-), multiplication (x), or division (÷)—you would use to solve each problem. You MAY need more than one operation!

1. There are * students in a class. There are * students in a row. How many rows are there?

_____

_____

2. John has * baseball cards. He traded * cards with Evan for * new cards. How many cards does he have after the trade?

_____

_____

3. Lynn saves quarters in a special bank. She has * quarters. How much money does she have?

_____

_____

4. Josh bought a package of gum drops. There were * orange, * red, * yellow, and * green ones in the package. How many gum drops were there in all?

_____

_____

5. June has * dollars. All of her money is in $5 bills. How many bills does she have?

_____

_____

Name _____ Date _____

**Exercise 2.18**

Suppose that * represents any number. Tell what operation—addition (+), subtraction (-), multiplication (x), or division (÷)—you would use to solve each problem. You MAY need more than one operation!

1. Sarah has * shirts and * pants that can all be worn together in combinations. How many outfits can she put together?

_____

_____

2. Jane has * dollars to spend at the mall. She buys a pair of jeans for * dollars and a new hair wrap for * dollars. She sees her grandmother, who gives her * dollars more. How much does she now have?

_____

_____

3. Dakota spends 50 cents a day on soda and snacks. In one week's time, Dakota buys * sodas and * snacks. How much is spent in one full week?

_____

_____

4. Ciara, Janis, and Aspen score *, *, and * on their final tests. What is their average score?

_____

_____

5. Willie gets paid * dollars an hour for painting at the school. Willie plans to work a total of * hours this summer. In addition to this, Willie plans to mow lawns * times at $7.00 a lawn. How much does Willie plan to earn this summer?

_____

_____

6. The Middle School Athletic Program receives 25 cents for every can of soda it sells. There are 24 cans in each case of soda. It sells * cases. How much will the Athletic Program make?

_____

_____

Name_____ Date _____

**Exercise 2.19**

Suppose that * represents any number. Tell what operation—addition (+), subtraction (-), multiplication (x), or division (÷)—you would use to solve each problem. You MAY need more than one operation!

1. Nickos works after school for * hours, three days each week. Nickos earns * dollars per hour. How much will Nickos earn each week?

_____

_____

2. Kaylin baby-sits for three children on Saturday mornings. Mom leaves * snacks. How many snacks will each child receive?

_____

_____

3. At the grocery store, Reilly buys six items totaling *. He pays with a $20 bill. How much change does Reilly get back if he also pays with a coupon for *?

_____

_____

4. Sean's church basement is crawling with crickets! Members of the yourth group are paid 5 cents for each cricket caught. Sean's youth group caught * crickets. How much were they paid?

_____

_____

5. The Smith family is going to the amusement park. They need two adult's tickets at * each and three children's tickets at * each. How much will it cost them to enter the park?

_____

_____

6. There are * rooms having * rows with * chairs in each row. How many chairs are there?

_____

_____

Name _____ Date _____

**Exercise 2.20**

Suppose that * represents any number. Tell what operation—addition (+), subtraction (-), multiplication (x), or division (÷)—you would use to solve each problem. You MAY need more than one operation!

1. Somebody really goofed! When the uniforms for the *-member marching band arrived, Nika noticed that none of the buttons had been sewn on properly. There are * buttons on each uniform. How many buttons had to be re-sewn?

   _____

   _____

2. The high school debate club is selling pencils before school every morning for * cents each. They sold * the first week, * the second week, and * the third week. How much have they made in three weeks?

   _____

   _____

3. Brendan, Vincent, and Kolby are collecting aluminum cans. For each pound of cans they collect, they are paid *. There are * pounds of cans collected so far. How much money have they made?

   _____

   _____

4. Mikayal and Allie are writing pages for the school newspaper. The newspaper is * pages long, and they have spent * hours writing. On average, how much time is spent writing each page?

   _____

   _____

5. DeCarlos has a budget of * dollars to buy plaques and medals. DeCarlos needs to order * medals at $3.00 each and * plaques at $10.00 each. Does he have enough money?

   _____

   _____

Name _____ Date _____

**Exercise 2.21**

Suppose that * represents any number. Tell what operation—addition (+), subtraction (-), multiplication (x), or division (÷)—you would use to solve each problem. You MAY need more than one operation!

1. Alice bowled * and *. What was her total score?

_____

_____

2. Each of five people on the team scored *. What was the team total?

_____

_____

3. On another night, the three highest scores were *, *, and *. What was the average score?

_____

_____

4. Each game was allowed 50 minutes of time. How many hours did it take to bowl * games?

_____

_____

5. Betty bowled a * on her first game and * on her second game. How many fewer points did she bowl on her second game?

_____

_____

6. Team scores were as follows: Team 1 = *, Team 2 = *, and Team 3 = *. How many points less than the average was Team 1?

_____

_____

Name_____ Date _____

**Exercise 2.22**

Many times you will need to use more than one operation to solve a problem. Circle the operations needed to solve the problem. Number the operations in the order they should be completed.

1. A class of 28 students decided to buy each of their four teachers flowers. Each floral arrangement costs $17.50, and the total cost would be shared equally by the students. How much money would each student owe?

       add            subtract          multiply         divide

2. Janna read six books with 72 pages each. It took her 11 days to read all the books. About how many pages did she read each day?

       add            subtract          multiply         divide

3. Aaron needs to write his 15 vocabulary words four times each. How many more than 50 words will he write?

       add            subtract          multiply         divide

4. Ninety plants were delivered to the local nursery. One-fourth of the plants sold the first day. How many plants are left?

       add            subtract          multiply         divide

5. Jacob's class is making butter. Each student shakes the jar of cream for exactly 25 seconds and then passes it immediately to the next student. If this process takes a total of 10 minutes, how many students are in Jacob's class?

       add            subtract          multiply         divide

6. Pete wants to run 100 miles this month. If he averages 4.25 miles each day for the first 15 days, how many more miles does he still need to run?

       add            subtract          multiply         divide

Name _____ Date _____

**Exercise 2.23**

Many times you will need to use more than one operation to solve a problem. Circle the operations needed to solve the problem. Number the operations in the order they should be completed.

1. Hannah does 46 pushups every day. Alice does eight more pushups than Hannah. What is their average?

           add               subtract            multiply            divide

2. Kurt needs to lift weights a total of 48 times to complete his summer goal. He lifts three times a week and has lifted 33 times so far. How many more weeks will he need to lift weights?

           add               subtract            multiply            divide

3. Stacy drives $1\frac{1}{2}$ hours during each outing with her instructor. She drives three times each week. She needs a total of 27 hours of driving time. How many weeks will this take?

           add               subtract            multiply            divide

4. Mr. Leach drinks three cans of diet soda each and every day. There are 24 cans of soda in a case. How many cases will Mr. Leach drink in eight weeks?

           add               subtract            multiply            divide

5. Julianne works from 8 to 11 at the middle school Monday through Friday. How many days will it take her to work a total of 51 hours?

           add               subtract            multiply            divide

# Step Three: Cooking

Now that the recipe has been carefully read, the ingredients have been precisely measured, and the mixing is accomplished, it is time to let it cook. Mathematicians "cook" when they find the answer using addition, subtraction, multiplication, and/or division.

## Perform the required operations and solve the equation.

## Do the math!

## Get the answer!

Name_____ Date _____

**Exercise 3.1**

Using order of operations is always an important ingredient in solving any mathematical equation. Let's practice some. (Remember: Do what is in the ( ) first, then the multiplication and division in the order they occur from left to right, and THEN do the addition and subtraction.)

1. $4 + 8 \times 2 - 7 =$

2. $9 \times 2 \div 3 + 7 - 5 =$

3. $5 - 3 \div 3 + 8 \times 3 =$

4. $16 \times 3 - 25 \div 5 + 1 =$

5. $9 - 48 \div 16 \times 2 - 1 =$

6. $3 (3 \times 7 + 2) - 10 \div 2 =$

7. $18 \div 6 \times 4 \div 2 + 4 =$

8. $8 + 5 - 7 + 6 \times 4 \div 2 =$

9. $4 \div 2 + 3 - 36 \div 18 =$

10. $20 \times 2 - 3 + 54 \div 9 =$

53

Name_____ Date _____

**Exercise 3.2**

Using the following information, solve these problems.

There are 180 school days in one year.
There are 365 days in one calendar year.
There are 52 weeks in one year.

| January 1999 | | | | | | |
| S | M | T | W | T | F | S |
|---|---|---|---|---|---|---|
| | | | | | 1 | 2 |
| 3 | 4 | 5 | 6 | 7 | 8 | 9 |
| 10 | 11 | 12 | 13 | 14 | 15 | 16 |
| 17 | 18 | 19 | 20 | 21 | 22 | 23 |
| 24/31 | 25 | 26 | 27 | 28 | 29 | 30 |

1. Emma is four years old. How many days old is she?

2. Jan studies 2.5 hours every night for school. How many hours does she spend studying after school in a year?

3. Keith has a part-time job. He works 1.5 hours each Tuesday and Thursday after school and throughout the summer. How many hours does he work in a year?

4. Becky practices piano a half hour after every weekday and two hours every weekend. How many hours does she spend practicing piano in a year?

5. Jacob plays about three hours of video games each week. How many hours has he spent playing video games in four years?

6. The Smiths spend every Saturday morning cleaning house. It takes them about $2\frac{1}{2}$ hours to complete all the work. How many hours do they spend cleaning house in two years?

Name_____ Date _____

**Exercise 3.3**

The local sports store is having a sale on all remaining baseball equipment.

| Baseball Pants | Striped Socks | Baseball Shoes |
|---|---|---|
| Reg. $9.99 | Reg. $7.99 | Reg. $34.99 |
| Now $7.99 | Now $4.99 | Now $22.99 |

| Youth Baseball Gloves | Batting Gloves | Baseball Bats |
|---|---|---|
| Reg. $39.99 | Reg. $7.99 | Reg. $33.99 |
| Now 15% off | Now $4.99 | Now 30% off |

1. How much more is the regular price of baseball shoes than the sale price?

2. What is the sale price of bats?

3. What is the amount saved on bats?

4. How much is the total bill for new pants, new socks, a pair of shoes, and a batting glove?

5. What is the sale price of a new baseball glove?

6. You have three $20 bills. Name two combinations of items you could purchase and still have between $15 and $25 left.

Name_____ Date _____

**Exercise 3.4**

At a recent town track meet, all ages competed in the long jump contest. A two-year-old jumped 1.32 feet. A five-year-old jumped 6.25 feet. A 10-year-old jumped 10.7 feet. A middle school student recorded a jump of 17.29 feet, while his pet frog leaped 11.88 feet.

1. What is the difference between the middle school student's jump and the 10-year-old's jump?

2. How many times greater was the frog's jump than the two-year-old's jump?

3. How much farther was the 10-year-old's jump than the five-year-old's jump?

4. How many equal jumps would the five-year-old need to make to cross a 125-foot field?

5. How many total feet did the jumps cover?

6. What is the sum of the two-year-old's jump, the middle school student's jump, and the frog's jump?

Name_____ Date _____

**Exercise 3.5**

This was the menu at our favorite fast food restaurant.

<u>ANY COMBO $2.99</u>

| **Combo A** | **Combo B** | **Combo C** | **Combo D** |
|---|---|---|---|
| $\frac{1}{4}$ lb. Hamburger | Roast Beef | Ham & Cheese | 2 Super Tacos |
| Large Fries | Large Fries | Large Fries | Nachos |
| Med. Drink | Med. Drink | Med. Drink | Med. Drink |

<u>REGULAR MENU</u>

$\frac{1}{4}$ lb. Hamburger  $1.79  with cheese $1.89
Roast Beef $1.89          Ham & Cheese  $1.79
Super Taco  $ .79          Fish  $1.79
Nachos $1.10              Fries  reg. $ .79  large $ .99
Drinks  small $ .79  medium $ .95  large $1.10

1. How much will I save by ordering Combo B instead of each item by itself?

2. How much do I save by ordering Combo C?

3. Which Combo is the BEST value?

4. How much could I expect to pay for one taco, nachos, and a medium drink?

5. What sandwich, fries/nacho, and drink combination could I order for over $4.00 if I did NOT order a Combo meal?

6. Is there any sandwich, fries/nacho, and drink combination that is cheaper than a combo meal?

Name _____ Date _____

**Exercise 3.6**

Solve the following problems.

1. The clock strikes its chimes every quarter hour. How many times will the clock chime in eight hours?

2. It is now 9:15 a.m. You got up 170 minutes ago. What time did you get up this morning?

3. It takes 25 minutes to do math homework, 30 minutes to do language arts, and 40 minutes to do science. You start working at 4:30 p.m. What time will it be when you complete your homework?

4. We left the school parking lot on our field trip to the zoo at 8:00 a.m. The bus drove 70 miles to get to the zoo and averaged a speed of 56 mph. At what time did we arrive?

5. A carpenter needs to assemble eight chairs and two tables. Each chair requires 20 minutes to assemble, and each table requires 45 minutes to assemble. The carpenter begins his work at 9:30 a.m. Did he finish assembling the chairs and tables in time for his 1:00 p.m. lunch break?

Name _____   Date _____

**Exercise 3.7**

Refer to the graph and answer the following questions.

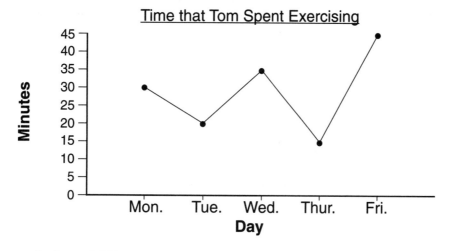

1. How much time did Tom spend exercising on Tuesday?

_____

2. How much time did Tom spend exercising on Thursday?

_____

3. How much more time did Tom spend exercising on Friday than on Monday?

_____

4. On what day did Tom spend the most time exercising?

_____

5. How much total time did he spend exercising Monday through Friday?

_____

6. How much time did he average each day?

_____

7. Tom exercised seven more minutes on Saturday than he did on Wednesday. How long did he exercise?

_____

8. The week before, Tom spent 40 minutes more time exercising. How many minutes did he exercise that week?

_____

9. What day did he spend the least time exercising?

_____

10. Next Monday, Tom will spend three times as much time exercising as he did on Thursday this week. How long will he exercise?

_____

Name _____ Date _____

**Exercise 3.8**

Grandpa Dean's Bakery is open five days every week. It is open exactly four weeks each month. In January, Grandpa Dean's Bakery sold 10 dozen doughnuts every day. In February, it sold 15 dozen every day. In March, it sold only nine dozen every day. In April, it sold twice as many per day as it did in January. How many dozen doughnuts did it sell in April?

1. What information is NOT needed to solve this problem?

_____

_____

_____

2. How many dozen doughnuts did it sell in April?

3. What was the average number of doughnuts sold daily from January through April?

4. Doughnuts sell for $2.00 a dozen. Make a chart showing how much money Grandpa Dean's Bakery collected on doughnuts each month.

Name_____ Date _____

**Exercise 3.9**

Jamie plans to use the following cookie recipe.

2 cups of sugar
$\frac{1}{2}$ cup margarine
5 Tablespoons of cocoa
$\frac{1}{2}$ cup milk
1 Tablespoon vanilla
$3\frac{3}{4}$ cups quick oats

Combine measured sugar, margarine, cocoa, and milk in a saucepan. Cook ingredients over heat until dissolved and mixture comes to a rolling boil. Let boil for one minute and then remove from heat. Add vanilla and oats, mixing thoroughly. Drop by teaspoon on waxed paper. Cool. Makes approximately four dozen cookies.

1. If there are 16 tablespoons to a cup, how many total cups of ingredients are in this recipe?

2. Jamie needs to make 12 dozen cookies for a church picnic. How much of each ingredient will she need?

3. Jamie needs to make six dozen cookies for a class party. How much of each ingredient will she need?

4. Jamie wants to make two dozen cookies for after-school snacks. How much of each ingredient will she need?

Name _____ Date _____

**Exercise 3.10**

Use this chart to solve the following problems.

| | | | **Number of Items Required** | | | | |
|---|---|---|---|---|---|---|---|
| **Item** | **Amount** | **Grade:** | **K-1** | **2-3** | **4-5** | **6** | **7** |
| Writing tablet | 75¢ each | | 1 | 2 | 2 | 3 | 4 |
| #2 pencils | 13¢ each or 2 for 25¢ | | 2 | 2 | 6 | 5 | 5 |
| folders | 25¢ each or 5 for $1.00 | | 2 | 3 | 6 | 6 | 6 |
| spiral notebook | 60¢ each | | 0 | 2 | 3 | 4 | 4 |
| ruler | 50¢ each | | 0 | 1 | 1 | 1 | 1 |
| pack of crayons | $1.50 each | | 1 | 1 | 1 | 1 | 1 |
| glue stick | 80¢ each | | 1 | 1 | 1 | 1 | 1 |
| scissors | 25¢ each | | 1 | 1 | 1 | 1 | 1 |
| ink pens | 25¢ each | | 0 | 0 | 1 | 2 | 3 |
| markers | $1.00 each | | 1 | 1 | 1 | 1 | 1 |

1. Emily will be starting kindergarten and her sister, Amy, will be starting the second grade. How much will their school supplies cost?

2. The twins will be entering grade four, and their brother, Andrew, will be starting grade seven. How much will their school supplies cost?

3. Michael will be entering third grade. He has a good pair of scissors, a ruler, and most of a glue stick. How much will his supplies cost?

4. If a family has seven children in grades K-6 (one child per grade), what would it cost for school supplies?

Name _____ Date _____

**Exercise 3.11**

Use the chart on Exercise 3.10, and solve these problems.

1. John will be starting the fifth grade. He has a good ruler and a pair of scissors. His crayons are still good, too. How much will his supplies cost?

2. Karin moved here over the summer and will start seventh grade. She has a writing tablet, scissors, one spiral notebook, and two pens she did not use from last year. How much will her supplies cost?

3. There are five children in the Amos family. Chad will be in kindergarten. Joe will start second grade. Chris will be in grade five. Alex will be in grade six, and Greg will be in seventh grade. Only Chad needs scissors. Joe, Alex, and Greg will need rulers. Nobody needs ink pens. How much will supplies cost?

4. What is the difference between the cost of supplies for a fifth grader and a seventh grader?

Name _____ Date _____

**Exercise 3.12**

Use the following information to solve these problems.

The Kidz Store is having a back-to-school clearance sale.

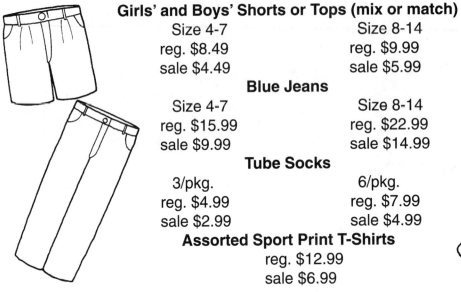

### Girls' and Boys' Shorts or Tops (mix or match)

| Size 4-7 | Size 8-14 |
|---|---|
| reg. $8.49 | reg. $9.99 |
| sale $4.49 | sale $5.99 |

### Blue Jeans

| Size 4-7 | Size 8-14 |
|---|---|
| reg. $15.99 | reg. $22.99 |
| sale $9.99 | sale $14.99 |

### Tube Socks

| 3/pkg. | 6/pkg. |
|---|---|
| reg. $4.99 | reg. $7.99 |
| sale $2.99 | sale $4.99 |

### Assorted Sport Print T-Shirts

reg. $12.99
sale $6.99

Tony needs a pair of blue jeans, three pairs of socks, one pair of shorts, and two tops. He wears size seven.

1. How much will his new clothes cost him?

2. How much will he save by buying his clothes on sale?

Tony's big brother, Al, needs two pairs of blue jeans, six pairs of socks, and two sport print T-shirts.

3. How much will his new clothes cost?

4. How much will he save by buying his clothes on sale?

Name _____ Date _____

**Exercise 3.13**

Use the prices listed in Exercise 3.12 to solve the following problems.

Twins Allen and Jesse need just shorts and tops. Each needs two pairs of shorts and three tops. Allen wears size 7, and Jesse wears size 8.

1. How much did their new clothes cost?

2. How much money did Allen save by buying his clothes on sale?

3. How much money did Jesse save by buying his clothes on sale?

4. What was the total amount Allen and Jesse saved?

5. Did they save enough for each to buy a pair of jeans and a sport print T-shirt?

6. Did they save enough for each to buy socks in addition to the items in #5? What size package might each buy?

Name _____ Date _____

**Exercise 3.14**

Use the following information to solve these problems.

**Grocery Store Prices**
1 lb. sliced ham $2.10 (10 slices)          Am. cheese $2.40 lb. (16 slices)
1 lb. sliced turkey breast $2.90 (10 slices)   $1\frac{1}{2}$ lb. loaf bread $1.25 (25 slices)

**Middle School Menu Prices**
milk—20 cents per carton                    chips—40 cents
snack cake—40 cents                         fruit—25 cents a piece
regular lunch (includes 1 carton milk)—$1.40

Mom usually packs sandwiches for Carla, Donna, and Joan's school lunches. Each girl has a sandwich (two slices of bread, a slice of meat, and a slice of cheese). They usually buy a carton of milk at school.

1. How much does it cost to make ham and cheese sandwiches for the three girls for one school week?

2. How much does it cost to make turkey and cheese sandwiches for the three girls for one school week?

3. How much does it cost to make each girl five sandwiches—three ham and cheese and two turkey and cheese—and to buy each girl milk, one piece of fruit, and chips or snack cake daily for one school week?

4. On Fridays, the girls like to eat school lunch. How much would it cost for five days of lunches if each girl skipped her regular ham and cheese, fruit, and snack (see problem #3) and had school lunch instead?

66

Name _____ Date _____

**Exercise 3.15**

Use the information from Exercise 3.14 to solve the following problems.

1. Greg usually eats two sandwiches (four slices of bread) each day for lunch. He likes to have one cheese sandwich and one turkey sandwich. He buys two cartons of milk each day. How much is the total cost of his lunch each day?

2. How much will lunch cost him for five school days?

3. When Greg eats school lunch, he always buys an extra carton of milk. If Greg eats school lunch on two days, how much will the total cost be?

4. Greg will bring his own lunch for three days and eat school lunch for two days. What is the total cost of lunch that school week? (Remember the milk!)

5. Greg's mom sprained her wrist and could not make his lunch for one whole week of school. How much will five school lunches cost him? (Remember the milk.)

Name _____ Date _____

**Exercise 3.16**

Use this information to solve the following problems.

     Tierra's church youth group is selling packages of cookies to raise money for a two-day snow camp in January. There are three kinds of cookies for sale: coco-chip, peanut butter, and sugar cookies. Each box sells for $2.75. Each box costs the youth group $1.60. There are 12 people in Tierra's group, and snow camp will cost each person $30.00.

  1. How much will it cost for the entire group to go to snow camp?

  2. How many boxes of cookies does the group need to sell to raise the money?

  3. How many boxes should each member sell?

  4. A church member donated $50.00 to the group for the trip. With this additional money, how many fewer boxes do they need to sell?

Name _____ Date _____

**Exercise 3.17**

Use this information to solve these problems.

        John came home from school and was starved. He decided to make some cookies and chose this recipe.

**Sugar Cookies**

| | |
|---|---|
| 1 cup shortening | 2 cups flour |
| 1 teaspoon vanilla | 1 teaspoon cream of tartar |
| ½ cup white sugar | 1 teaspoon baking soda |
| ½ cup brown sugar | 1 teaspoon salt |
| 1 egg | |

1. If three teaspoons equal one Tablespoon and there are 16 Tablespoons in one cup, how many total Tablespoons are in this recipe? (Do NOT count the egg.)

2. If John uses two cups of shortening, how much brown sugar will he need to measure?

3. If John makes a "batch" using six cups of flour, how many teaspoons of cream of tartar will he need to measure?

4. John plans to make one and a half batches of cookies. How much white sugar will he need?

5. This recipe makes six dozen cookies. He wants to freeze four dozen, give three dozen to his teacher, take seven dozen to basketball practice, and have a dozen to keep in his cookie jar. How many batches should he make?

Name _____ Date _____

**Exercise 3.18**

Use this recipe to answer the following questions.

### Spice Tea

1 cup instant tea
$1\frac{1}{2}$ cups sugar
$1\frac{1}{2}$ cups instant pre-sweetened orange breakfast drink
$\frac{1}{2}$ cup pre-sweetened lemonade drink mix
$1\frac{3}{4}$ teaspoons cinnamon
$\frac{3}{4}$ teaspoon ginger
$\frac{1}{2}$ teaspoon ground cloves

Mix and store dry ingredients in a jar. Use three teaspoons of mix per cup of hot water for one serving of Spice Tea.

Three teaspoons equal one Tablespoon, and there are 16 Tablespoons in one cup.

1. How many total Tablespoons of ingredients are there in this recipe?

2. How many total servings does this recipe make?

3. If you double this recipe, how much of each ingredient will you need?

4. If you want to use $1\frac{1}{2}$ cups of instant tea, how much of each of the other ingredients would you use?

Name _____ Date _____

**Exercise 3.19**

Use the following information to complete these problems.

| Item | Serving Size | Calories | Calories From Fat |
|------|--------------|----------|-------------------|
| Vanilla wafers | 8 | 130 | 40 |
| Chicken snack crackers | 11 | 160 | 80 |
| Angel food cake | 1 slice* | 140 | 0 |
| Wheat cracker with cheese | 4 | 140 | 70 |
| Peanut butter bar | 1 | 290 | 140 |
| Shoestring potato sticks | 1 serv.** | 150 | 90 |
| Striped shortbread cookies | 2 | 140 | 70 |

*One slice is considered $\frac{1}{12}$ of an entire cake.
**One serving is considered $\frac{2}{3}$ cup.

    Stephanie, Samantha, and Josie choose snacks every day after they get off the bus. In one week's time, Stephanie chose 12 vanilla wafers, one slice of angel food cake, one peanut butter bar, and one serving of shoestring potatoes. Samantha chose 11 chicken snack crackers, nine striped shortbread cookies, one peanut butter bar, and one slice of angel food cake. Josie chose 10 wheat crackers with cheese, one slice of angel food cake, one serving of shoestring potatoes, and two striped shortbread cookies.

1. How many calories and how many fat calories did each consume?

    **Stephanie**        **Samantha**        **Josie**

2. List the girls in order from highest to lowest calories consumed.

3. How many more did the highest calorie consumer eat than the lowest calorie consumer?

Name _____ Date _____

**Exercise 3.20**

Use the following information to complete these problems.

The local grocery store has weekly specials. This week, they have these.

| Item | Amount | Sale Price | Regular Price |
|---|---|---|---|
| Red or white seedless grapes | 1 lb. | 89¢ | $1.25 |
| Iced cinnamon rolls | 1 dozen | $1.49 | $2.75 |
| Nectarines | 1 lb. | 99¢ | $1.45 |
| Strawberries | 2 lb. | $3.00 | $4.00 |
| Sandwich bread | 1 lb. loaf | 99¢ | $1.29 |
| Peaches | 1 lb. | 99¢ | $1.39 |
| Eggs (medium) | 1 dozen | 19¢ | 45¢ |
| Ground beef | 3 lb. pack | 97¢/lb. | $1.39/lb. |
| Bag cereal | 2 bags | $3.00 | $3.75 |

1. Carol bought these groceries on sale this week: one pound grapes, two loaves bread, one dozen eggs, three pounds ground beef, and two bags of cereal. How much less did she pay for these groceries this week than she paid for them last week when they were not on sale?

2. Helen is making a special fruit salad and needs to buy one pound of white grapes, two pounds of peaches, two pounds of strawberries, and one pound of nectarines. How much does she save by buying the ingredients this week as compared to buying them at the regular prices?

3. Lauren, Sammi, and Tia are sleeping over at CorDelia's house. CorDelia wants to buy two pounds of strawberries, one bag of cereal, and one dozen iced cinnamon rolls for breakfast. What will be the average cost per person?

Name_____ Date _____

**Exercise 3.21**

Use the following chart to complete these problems.

| Item | Size | Number of Calories |
|------|------|--------------------|
| Apple | 1 average | 61 |
| Apricots | 3 fresh | 55 |
| Bagel | 1, 3 in. diameter | 165 |
| Banana | 1 | 118 |
| Carrot sticks | 1 whole carrot | 21 |
| Celery sticks | 1, 8 in. stalk | 7 |
| Grapes (white seedless) | 10 | 34 |
| Nectarine | 1, $2\frac{1}{2}$ in. diameter | 88 |
| Orange | 1 fresh | 71 |
| Peach | 1 fresh | 38 |
| Pear (Bartlett) | 1, $2\frac{1}{2}$ in. diameter | 100 |
| Raisins (seedless) | $\frac{1}{2}$ cup | 210 |
| Strawberries (fresh, whole) | $\frac{1}{2}$ cup | 28 |
| Tangerine (fresh) | 1 | 39 |

1. If Marla eats a bagel and a nectarine, how many calories has she consumed?

2. How many fewer calories would she have consumed if she had eaten three apricots instead of the bagel?

3. Ashton is having two friends over for lunch. She will make individual fruit salads. Each salad will consist of 10 seedless white grapes, one orange (sliced), one cup of fresh strawberries, and an apple (chopped). How many calories does each salad have?

4. Devlin wants to plan two snacks he can have that total 50 calories or less. Name six combinations he could use.

5. Rico needs to plan two snacks that total 300 calories or more. Name three combinations he could use.

Name _____ Date _____

**Exercise 3.22**

Darius bought items at Mr. Edgar's garage sale. He bought a picture frame for 50 cents, a dictionary for $2.60, a video tape for $1.49, a joke book for 35 cents, a baseball bat for $2.55, and a potted plant for 79 cents.

1. What is his total bill?

2. All his money is in one dollar bills. How many will he give Mr. Edgar?

3. How much change will Mr. Edgar give Darius?

4. In the chart below, list several ways Mr. Edgar could give Darius his change. (List at LEAST five ways, please.)

| Quarters | Dimes | Nickels | Pennies |
| --- | --- | --- | --- |
| _____ | _____ | _____ | _____ |
| _____ | _____ | _____ | _____ |
| _____ | _____ | _____ | _____ |
| _____ | _____ | _____ | _____ |
| _____ | _____ | _____ | _____ |
| _____ | _____ | _____ | _____ |

Name _____ Date _____

**Exercise 2.23**

Cortez and Remo shop the clearance racks at a local mall to find the best buys. They are excellent shoppers! They find and purchase the following sale-priced items:

- a jacket for $5.00 (reg. priced at $15.00)
- a beach towel for $3.49 (reg. priced at $8.50)
- a baseball cap for $2.88 (reg. priced at $7.99)
- a pair of swim trunks for $3.75 (reg. priced at $10.00)
- a short and shirt set for $9.99 (reg. priced at $20.00)
- a stretch belt for 57¢ (reg. priced at $6.00)

1. What is their total bill?

2. If the boys took two $20 bills to the mall with them, how much change will they receive?

3. List five ways the clerk could give Cortez and Remo the correct change.

Name _____ Date _____

**Exercise 3.24**

Mr. and Mrs. Walker are landscaping their new home. The local nursery lists these prices.

| Trees | Price |
| --- | --- |
| Red Maple | $24.99 |
| Pin Oaks | $14.99 |
| Japanese Maple | $39.99 |
| Elm | $14.99 |
| Dogwood | $21.99 |

| Shrubs | Price |
| --- | --- |
| Yews | $17.99 |
| Alberta Spruce | $24.99 |
| Bird Nest Spruce | $17.99 |
| Barberry | $8.99 |

1. How much will it cost them to buy one Japanese maple, five yews, three barberry bushes, two pin oaks, and three red maple trees?

2. Can they purchase two more trees and still stay under $300.00? If so, what two trees could they buy?

3. They may choose to buy two Alberta spruces in place of the Japanese maple and two barberry bushes instead of three barberry bushes. Will this be more or less expensive?

4. Find one combination of three trees and five shrubs that would cost less than $150.00. You must choose at least two different types of trees and at least two different types of shrubs.

# Step Four: Tasting

Tasting is the best part of cooking! It can also be the most exciting, because things may not turn out the way you expected. Word problems can be surprising, too. When the answer does not meet your expectations, you will need to decide where the mistake occurred. Was it in …

## Step One

Did you copy the facts correctly?
Did you get the facts straight?
Did you use information you did not need?

## Step Two

Did you mix the facts correctly with the necessary operation
or combination of operations?

## Step Three

Did you have a "cooking" problem or an error in doing the math?

You may want to use estimation to see if your answer "tastes good"
or if it belongs in the garbage!

(or in a galaxy far, **far away!!!**)

  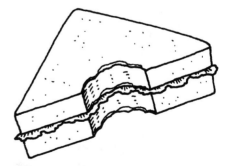

Name _____ Date _____

**Exercise 4.1**

Does your answer make sense? Choose a reasonable answer for each.

1. The length of a kitchen table

   a. 28 inches
   b. 3 yards
   c. 6 feet
   d. 300 inches

2. The height of a car

   a. 48 inches
   b. 20 inches
   c. 70 inches
   d. 100 inches

3. The gallons of gas needed to travel 100 miles

   a. 100 gallons
   b. 40
   c. 2 gallons
   d. 5 gallons

4. Cups of water needed to fill a two-quart pitcher

   a. 8
   b. 2
   c. 25
   d. 12

5. The time it takes to walk three miles

   a. 60 minutes
   b. 10 minutes
   c. 35 minutes
   d. 3 minutes

**HOUSTON**
**100 miles**

Name _____  Date _____

**Exercise 4.2**

Does your answer make sense? Choose a reasonable answer for each.

1. The weight of a math book

   a. 5 lbs.
   b. 10 lbs.
   c. 2 lbs.
   d. 7 lbs.

2. The height of a room's ceiling

   a. 20 ft.
   b. 3 ft.
   c. 8 ft.
   d. 15 ft.

3. The length of a football

   a. 30 cm
   b. 1 meter
   c. 12 cm
   d. 50 mm

4. The length of a school bus

   a. 12 ft.
   b. 40 ft.
   c. 120 yards
   d. 35 yards

5. The weight of a dictionary

   a. 3 lbs.
   b. 6 lbs.
   c. 8 lbs.
   d. 10 lbs.

Name _____ Date _____

**Exercise 4.3**

Does your answer make sense? Choose a reasonable answer for each.

1. The amount of punch to serve eight children

   a. 2 milliliters
   b. 2 liters
   c. 10 milliliters
   d. 10 liters

2. The mass of a dime

   a. 3 grams
   b. 3 kilograms
   c. 17 grams
   d. 8 kilograms

3. The length of a swimming pool

   a. 15 mm
   b. 15 cm
   c. 15 m
   d. 15 km

4. The mass of a granola bar

   a. 35 g
   b. 1 kg
   c. 75 g
   d. 4 g

5. The length of a comb

   a. 12 mm
   b. 12 cm
   c. 12 m
   d. 12 km

Name _____  Date _____

**Exercise 4.4**

Does your answer make sense? Choose a reasonable answer for each.

1. The length of a rubber band

   a. 4 mm
   b. 4 cm
   c. 4 m
   d. 4 km

2. The mass of an infant

   a. 4 g
   b. 10 g
   c. 4 kg
   d. 10 kg

3. The amount of medicine in a teaspoon

   a. 5 mL
   b. 5 L
   c. 20 mL
   d. 20 L

4. The mass of a frozen pizza

   a. 17 g
   b. 500 g
   c. 7 kg
   d. 3 kg

5. The length of a shoe lace

   a. 7 cm
   b. 20 cm
   c. 70 cm
   d. 7 m

Name_____ Date _____

**Exercise 4.5**

The Taylor family wants to check in at a local motel. The motel posts room rates at the front desk. Use the chart to determine if the check-in clerk's response is reasonable in each case. If it is not, explain what the correct answer should be.

**Rates Per Night**

| | |
|---|---|
| 1 person | $39.00 |
| 2 persons | $45.00 |
| 2 persons, 2 beds | $49.00 |
| 3 persons, 2 beds | $55.00 |
| 4 persons, 2 beds | $59.00 |
| cots and baby beds | $10.00 |

1. Mr. Taylor asks for the cost of a room for three people for two nights. The clerk says it will be $147.00.

_____

_____

2. Mr. Taylor asks for the cost for four people to rent a room for three nights. They will also need a bed for their baby. The clerk says it will cost $207.00.

_____

_____

3. Mr. Taylor asks how much it will cost for two people to rent a room with two beds for five nights. The clerk says it will cost about $300.00.

_____

_____

4. Mr. Taylor says he will need a room for three nights. The clerk says it will cost $135.00.

_____

_____

5. Mr. Taylor asks how much it will cost for two adults and one child to rent a one-bed room with a cot for two nights. The clerk says it will cost $110.00.

_____

_____

Name _____ Date _____

**Exercise 4.6**

Use the chart to determine if the bill is reasonable or unreasonable in each case. Explain your answers.

### Buffet Prices

| | |
|---|---|
| Adults (12 yrs. and up) | $7.95 |
| Children (5–11 yrs. old) | $3.95 |
| Sr. Citizens (55 yrs. and up) | $5.95 |
| Soup/Salad Bar only | $3.95 |
| Dessert Bar only | $2.95 |

All prices include beverage and tax.

1. Roxie, Calvin, Tasha, LaMar, and their grandparents ate at the buffet. The children (all under 12 years old) ate the regular buffet. Their grandparents had the soup/salad bar. The bill was about $24.00.

   _____

   _____

2. The Harris family treated Aunt Neva to lunch to celebrate her sixtieth birthday. The Harris children (ages 6 and 8) both ate the regular buffet along with the adults. The bill was about $30.00.

   _____

   _____

3. After leaving the movie, Chad and Heather decided to join their high school friends, Trey and Cherelle and Jordan and Natalie, at the buffet. Heather and Natalie want the dessert bar only. Cherelle chooses the soup/salad bar. The guys decide to eat the regular buffet. They have $32.00. Do they have enough money?

   _____

   _____

4. Sloan, Travis, Rob, and their parents decide to celebrate their making the honor roll in grades two, four, and eight. Mom and Dad ate the regular buffet. The kids all want the soup/salad bar and the dessert bar. The bill was about $37.00.

   _____

   _____

Name_____ Date _____

**Exercise 4.7**

Use estimation to decide if each situation is reasonable or not. Explain your answers.

**Bowling Alley Prices**

| | |
|---|---|
| Games | $1.75 each |
| Shoe rental | $1.50 |
| Drinks | sm. 50¢    lg. $1.00 |
| All snack items | 75¢ each |

1. Gabe has time to rent shoes and bowl only one game. Dad gives hims a $5 bill. The clerk gives him less than a dollar in change.

_____

_____

_____

2. Clint, Devlin, and Ray each have $10.00. Each plans to bowl three games, rent shoes, and have a large drink and two snacks.

_____

_____

_____

3. Chelten rents shoes and bowls three games. She decides to treat Chelsi, Addie, and herself to small drinks. Chelten started out with $10.00.

_____

_____

_____

4. Lance and Uncle Chaddrick challenge Marli and Aunt Paige to bowl three games. All four need to rent shoes. The losing team will buy large drinks for everyone. Each team has $20.00.

_____

_____

_____

Name _____ Date _____

**Exercise 4.8**

Practice your estimation skills by rounding the numbers below as directed.

Round to the nearest hundredth.

1) 14.826 _____        2) 4.587 _____

3) 22.498 _____        4) 9.723 _____

5) 0.265 _____         6) 5.016 _____

7) 38.614 _____        8) 6.623 _____

Round to the nearest tenth.

9) 26.78 _____         10) 37.14 _____

11) 7.57 _____         12) 82.62 _____

13) 4.52 _____         14) 63.67 _____

15) 10.072 _____       16) 246.86 _____

Round to the nearest whole number.

17) 235.095 _____      18) 321.499 _____

19) 36.85 _____        20) 2.697 _____

21) 0.49 _____         22) 10.582 _____

23) 49.9 _____         24) 300.75 _____

Round to the nearest hundred.

25) 1,468.03 _____     26) 735.542 _____

27) 992.9 _____        28) 5,249 _____

29) 8,764.29 _____     30) 627.9 _____

Name _____ Date _____

**Exercise 4.9**

Round each number to the nearest whole number, then add or subtract.

1)  47.69
  + 83.51

2)  947.49
  + 638.32

3)  48.62
  − 37.80

4)  9.369
  − 6.475

Round each number to the largest place value, then multiply.

5)  28
  x  7

6)  297
  x  3

7)  381
  x  23

8)  65
  x  41

Round each number to the nearest tenth, then multiply.

9)  29.54
  x      6

10)  7.284
  x      7

11)  922.06
  x      3

Round each fraction to the nearest whole number, then add.

12) $\frac{3}{4} + \frac{1}{5} =$ _____

13) $\frac{13}{20} + \frac{7}{8} =$ _____

14)  $5\frac{2}{3}$
  + $6\frac{1}{8}$

15)  $4\frac{8}{9}$
  + $9\frac{2}{3}$

# Answer Keys

### Exercise 1.1 (page 4)
Students do NOT need to know:
1) The triplets ate four eggs, eight strips of bacon, and six slices of toast.
2) Jane ate 12 cookies and Mom ate four cookies.
3) There are 427 potato chips in the bag and how long it took each to eat their chips.
4) Karin made six slices of cinnamon toast.
5) Phil ate 12 total squares of pizza and that three squares were ham.
6) Heather and Chad ate three boxes of popcorn, Nathan ate one soft pretzel, and Bob ate two boxes of popcorn.

### Exercise 1.2 (page 5)
Students do NOT need to know:
1) Abby gets paid $20 a week, three neighbors pay cash, and two neighbors pay by check.
2) Three neighbors pay cash, two neighbors pay every week, two neighbors pay by check, two neighbors pay once a month, and one neighbor pays every other week.
3) The price of tickets is $3.50.
4) The bikes are 10, 15, and 18 speeds and how fast the bikes are traveling.
5) Oranges are 40 cents each.
6) The number of boys she had each year

### Exercise 1.3 (page 6)
Students still NEED to know:
1) How many pieces of felt were in the large box?
2) No more information is needed.
3) No more information is needed.
4) How much the package of socks cost?
5) How many people are in the group?

### Exercise 1.4 (page 7)
Students still NEED to know:
1) How much was spent on equipment?
2) How much did the pictures cost each member?
3) No more information is needed.
4) How many players are on the team?
5) How many total pages or books are required?

### Exercise 1.5 (page 8)
Answers (pictures) may vary.
PROBLEM 1

|          | blue | green | red | black |
|----------|------|-------|-----|-------|
| 8 mittens | 5    | 2     | 1   | 0     |
| 3 boots  | 1    | 0     | 0   | 2     |
| 7 hats   | 3    | 1     | 2   | 1     |

There are 18 children in all.
Blue items total 9.
Red items total 3.

### PROBLEM 2
a) 30 divided by 8 is 3, with a remainder of 6. So, 4 tables are needed.
b) The 2 end tables will have 7 children each.
   50 - 14 = 36
   The middle tables will have 6 children each.
   36 ÷ 6 = 6
   So, a total of 8 tables are needed.

### PROBLEM 3
The fewest number of triangles that an eight-sided figure may be divided into is six.

### Exercise 1.6 (page 9)
Answers (pictures) may vary.
PROBLEM 1
   Yes, there is enough room.
   4 x 3 = 12, 5 x 2 = 10, 3 x 3 = 9
   and 12 + 10 + 9 = 31
PROBLEM 2
   Yes, there is enough room.
   2 x 6 = 12, 3 x 4 = 12, 3 x 3 = 9
   and 12 + 12 + 9 = 33
PROBLEM 3
   1 x 5 = 5, 3 x 4 = 12, 5 + 12 = 17, so there are 10 children remaining. These 10 could be divided into 2 groups of 3 and 2 groups of 2 OR 5 groups of 2.

### Exercise 1.7 (page 10)
Answers (pictures) may vary.
PROBLEM 1
```
X X X X X X X
1 2 3 4 5 6 7 8
```

There is 12 cm between #2 and #6.

PROBLEM 2
```
X X X X X X X X X X X X X X
1 2 3 4 5 6 7 8 9 10 11 12 13 14
```

There is 72 feet between #3 and #11.

PROBLEM 3

There is a total of 98 cm.

PROBLEM 4

-X-X-X-X-X-X-X-X-X-X-X-X-X-X-X-X-X-X-X-X-X-

This leaves 21 spaces of 6 inches each for a total of 126 inches.

        

PROBLEM 5

Top

Middle

Bottom

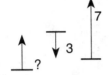

Middle to Top is 4 stories, so the building is 8 stories tall.

## Exercise 1.8 (page 11)
Answers (pictures) will vary.
1) Kite 1 = 400 feet
   Kite 2 is $\frac{1}{2}$ of 400 feet = 200 feet
   Kite 3 is $\frac{1}{5}$ of 400 feet = 80 feet

2) Bill = 2
   Mark = 1
   Keith = 4
   Joe = 3
   They mowed a total of 10 lawns.
   $70 divided by 10 = $7 per lawn.

3) They need to know the Pythagorean Triangle Identity.
   $30^2 + 40^2 = 900 + 1600$
   $= 2500$
   $= 50^2$

4) 3 times 4 = 12 outfits

## Exercise 1.9 (page 12)
Answers (pictures) will vary.
1) Each person will give to the other 4 people, so 5 times 4, or 20, gifts will be exchanged.

2) Each person will give to the other 9 people, so 10 times 9, or 90, gifts will be exchanged.

## Exercise 1.10 (page 13)
Answers (pictures) will vary.
1) With meat and bread there are 2 x 3, or 6, combinations. Each of these may go with just lettuce or just cheese or just tomato or lettuce/cheese or lettuce/tomato or cheese/tomato or lettuce/cheese/tomato or none. This then gives 6 x 8, or 48, combinations.

2) He may choose 3 ice creams with topping A only, B only, C only, A & B, B & C, A & C, A & B & C, or no topping at all. This gives 3 x 8, or 24, combinations. He then may choose whipped cream, nuts, both, or nothing on each of these 24 combinations for a total of 24 x 4, or 96, possible combinations.

## Exercise 1.11 (page 14)
Charts will vary.
1) Jenny: Grape
   John: Lemon-Lime
   Janna: Orange
   Jarret: Cola

2) Jenny: Vacuum
   John: Trash
   Janna: Dust
   Jarret: Clean Sinks

## Exercise 1.12 (page 15)
Charts will vary.
1) Ann: 2nd place
   Sue: No ribbon
   Joy: 3rd place
   Dot: 1st place

2) Ann: 5 events
   Sue: 2 events
   Joy: 3 events
   Dot: 4 events

## Exercise 1.13 (page 16)
Charts will vary.
1) Al: Curls
   Bob: Squats
   Carl: Military Press
   Dale: Toe Raises
   Evan: Lateral Pull Downs
   George: Bench Press

2) Sally: white
   Rachel: yellow
   Fred: green
   Zane: blue

## Exercise 1.14 (page 17)
Charts will vary.
1) Sarah: Blueberry
   Emily: Orange
   Alwin: Cherry
   Rick: Grape
   Sharon: Lime
2) Sarah: Bedroom
   Emily: Bathroom
   Alwin: Living Room
   Rick: Office
   Sharon: Kitchen

## Exercise 1.15 (page 18)
Claire: 2nd Base
Michelle: Center Field
Tracy: Left Field
Jenny: Catcher
Elaine: Right Field
Janna: Short Stop
Rachel: 3rd Base
Whitney: Pitcher
Kari: 1st Base

## Exercise 1.16 (page 19)
1) 2 and 6
2) 2 and 7
3) 3
4) 1, 4, and 8
5) 2
6) 6
7) 4

## Exercise 1.17 (page 20)
Teacher check diagram.
1) 1
2) 3
3) 6
4) 10
5) 14

## Exercise 1.18 (page 21)
Teacher check diagrams.
1) 6 students
2) 4 students

## Exercise 1.19 (page 22)
1) Highest:   Mona
              Carol
              Wanda
   Lowest:    Beth

2) Most missed:  Will
                  Ben
                  Glen
   Least missed:  Andy

3) First place: Raymond
                Mike
                Jay
                Richard
                Dale
   Last place: Colin

### Exercise 1.20 (page 23)
1) Last team:  Panthers
              Eagles
              Warriors
   First team:  Tigers

2) Highest score:  Sue
                  Bob
                  Tim
   Lowest score:  Ellen

3) Most cards:  Kent
                Jack
                Mary
                Jade
   Least cards:  Sam

### Exercise 1.21 (page 24)
1) Longest streak: Sharks
                Vikings
                Renegades
   Shortest streak: Bears

2) First winner:  Mike
                Joe
                Annette
   Last winner:  Barb

3) Smallest gym:  Brownsville
                Springfield
                Davis City
   Largest gym:  Carlton

### Exercise 1.22 (page 25)
1) Largest snowfall: Oak Hill
                Fulton
                Twin Falls
   Smallest snowfall: Maple

2) Most absences:  Armond
                  Hayley
                  Stonee
   Least absences:  Catlin

3) Lowest golf score:  Jamario
                    Shelby
                    Desiree
                    Ivan
   Highest golf score:  Marcus

### Exercise 1.23 (page 26)
1) First place:  Belleview
               Lenox
               Salem
   4th place:  Freeburg
2) First place:  Spencer
               Antonio
               Skylar
               Terrence
               Montel
   6th place:  London

3) Most recent:  Tyrus
               Dante
               Molly
               Kelsey

### Exercise 2.1 (page 28)
1) $168 + 947 + 89 = 1,204$
2) $82 + 93 + 87 = 262$
3) $87.9 + 6.73 + 4.08 = 98.71$
4) $\$4.27 + \$16.28 + \$47.92 + \$32.59 = \$101.06$
5) $8,746 + 96,487 = 105,233$
6) $8.9 + 4.7 + 63.8 = 77.4$

### Exercise 2.2 (page 29)
1) $48,387 + 3,580 + 259 = 52,226$
2) $87.4 + 86.2 + 39.2 + 79.5 = 292.3$
3) $81.29 + 64 + 0.47 = 145.76$
4) $\$16.47 + \$227.18 + \$1.63 = \$245.28$
5) $\$47.99 + \$52.12 + \$6.50 + \$12.69 = \$119.30$
6) $15,320 + 620 + 547 + 12 = 16,499$
7) $12.7 + 63.9 + 45 + 0.51 = 122.11$

### Exercise 2.3 (page 30)
1) $\frac{2}{5} + \frac{3}{4} + \frac{1}{2} = \frac{33}{20}$ or $1\frac{13}{20}$
2) $0.14 + 26.7 + 6.032 + 28 = 60.872$
3) $\frac{4}{9} + \frac{2}{3} + \frac{1}{4} = \frac{49}{36}$ or $1\frac{13}{36}$
4) $0.07 + 0.007 + 0.014 = 0.091$
5) $\frac{2}{3} + \frac{3}{4} + \frac{3}{5} = \frac{121}{60}$ or $2\frac{1}{60}$
6) $\$.75 + \$.97 + \$.55 + \$1.23 = \$3.50$

### Exercise 2.4 (page 31)
1) $9,118 - 4,381 = 4,737$
2) $15,384 - 6,154 = 9,230$
3) $82 - 28 = 54$
4) $20 - 8.2 = 11.8$
5) $78 - 39 = 39$
6) $673 - 486 = 187$
7) $\$100.00 - \$82.16 = \$17.84$

### Exercise 2.5 (page 32)
1) $826.4 - 59.63 = 766.77$
2) $68.05 - 4.0372 = 64.0128$
3) $10.01 - 6.4 = 3.61$
4) $81.9 - 17.58 = 64.32$
5) $\$10.00 - \$6.29 = \$3.71$
6) $0.01 - 0.001 = 0.009$
7) $\$1,000.00 - \$13.25 = \$986.75$

### Exercise 2.6 (page 33)
1) $\frac{5}{16} - \frac{7}{12} = \frac{13}{48}$
2) $\frac{25}{27} - \frac{1}{4} = \frac{73}{108}$
3) $\frac{11}{13} - \frac{3}{14} = \frac{115}{182}$
4) $\frac{6}{7} - \frac{3}{8} = \frac{27}{56}$
5) $\frac{8}{9} - \frac{1}{7} = \frac{47}{63}$
6) $\frac{5}{6} - \frac{5}{14} = \frac{40}{84} = \frac{10}{21}$

### Exercise 2.7 (page 35)
1) $167 + 52 = 219$
2) $7.59 - 6.8 = 0.79$
3) $1,000 - 864 = 136$
4) $37 + 9,642 = 9,679$
5) $368 - 2.5 = 365.5$
6) $597 + 48 = 645$
7) $9,654 + 163 = 9,817$
8) $40.06 - 13.14 = 26.92$

### Exercise 2.8 (page 36)
1) $\frac{13}{14} + \frac{2}{3} = \frac{67}{42}$ or $1\frac{25}{42}$
2) $\frac{7}{6} + \frac{5}{8} = \frac{43}{24}$ or $1\frac{19}{24}$
3) $1\frac{2}{5} - \frac{1}{4} = 1\frac{3}{20}$
4) $\frac{8}{9} - \frac{1}{7} = \frac{47}{63}$
5) $1.482 + 0.07 = 1.552$
6) $2.7 - 0.14 = 2.56$
7) $61 - 0.49 = 60.51$
8) $16.9 + 3.01 = 19.91$

### Exercise 2.9 (page 37)
1) $0.35 \times 80 = 28$
2) $0.40 \times 60 = 24$
3) $0.28 \times 50 = 14$
4) $0.30 \times 90 = 27$
5) $0.54 \times 160 = 86.4$
6) $0.76 \times 300 = 228$
7) $\frac{1}{3} \times 63 = 21$
8) $\frac{1}{5} \times 75 = 15$

9) $\frac{3}{4}$ x 60 = 45
10) $\frac{2}{7}$ x 77 = 22
11) $\frac{5}{6}$ x 48 = 40
12) $\frac{1}{8}$ x 56 = 7

## Exercise 2.10 (page 38)
1) 8 x 25 = 200
2) 39 x 16 = 624
3) 72 x 3 = 216
4) 14 x 12 = 168
5) 21 x 3 = 63
6) 46 x 12 = 552
7) 17 x 28 = 476
8) $\frac{2}{5}$ x 30 = 12
9) $\frac{1}{2}$ x $\frac{2}{3}$ = $\frac{2}{6}$ = $\frac{1}{3}$
10) $\frac{1}{4}$ x $\frac{5}{6}$ = $\frac{5}{24}$
11) $\frac{3}{4}$ x 62 = $\frac{93}{2}$ or $46\frac{1}{2}$
12) $\frac{1}{2}$ x 56 = 28
13) $8\frac{1}{2}$ x 6 = 51
14) $3\frac{1}{6}$ x 12 = 38

## Exercise 2.11 (page 39)
1) 182 ÷ 7 = 26
2) 672 ÷ 16 = 42
3) 5,270 ÷ 85 = 62
4) 356 ÷ 4 = 89
5) 4,425 ÷ 59 = 75
6) 16 ÷ $\frac{6}{7}$ = $\frac{56}{3}$ or $18\frac{2}{3}$
7) 9,672 ÷ 3 = 3,224

## Exercise 2.12 (page 40)
1) 1,628 ÷ 37 = 44
2) 2,660 ÷ 28 = 95
3) 252 ÷ 6 = 42
4) 1,005 ÷ 15 = 67
5) 1,792 ÷ 28 = 64
6) 343 ÷ 7 = 49
7) 384 ÷ 12 = 32

## Exercise 2.13 (page 41)
1) 13.364 ÷ 0.26 = 51.4
2) 27.48 ÷ 6 = 4.58
3) 3.87 ÷ 0.45 = 8.6
4) 45.44 ÷ 8 = 5.68
5) $\frac{4}{9}$ ÷ $\frac{2}{7}$ = $\frac{14}{9}$ or $1\frac{5}{9}$
6) $\frac{17}{80}$ ÷ $\frac{1}{4}$ = $\frac{17}{20}$
7) 20 ÷ $\frac{4}{9}$ = 45

## Exercise 2.14 (page 42)
1) 200 - 87 = 113
2) $4.48 + $13.56 + $.76 = $18.80
3) 27.2 ÷ 4 = 6.8
4) 46.7 + 18.9 = 65.6

5) 0.30 x 92 = 27.6
6) 54.027 ÷ 8.7 = 6.21
7) $10.00 - $7.52 = $2.48
8) 8.7 + 0.02 + 96 + 0.254 = 104.974

## Exercise 2.15 (page 43)
1) 82 - 2.8 = 79.2
2) $\frac{1}{3}$ x 225 = 85
3) 879 + 276 + 14,128 = 15,283
4) 343 ÷ 7 = 49
5) 0.29 x 53 = 15.37
6) 179.46 - 28.001 = 151.459
7) 3.268 ÷ 0.43 = 7.6
8) $\frac{2}{9}$ + $\frac{1}{6}$ + $\frac{2}{3}$ = $\frac{19}{18}$ or $1\frac{1}{18}$

## Exercise 2.16 (page 44)
1) $\frac{2}{5}$ + $\frac{7}{10}$ + $\frac{3}{20}$ + $\frac{3}{4}$ = $\frac{8}{5}$ or $1\frac{3}{5}$
2) 115.7 ÷ 13 = 8.9
3) 0.27 x 34 = 9.18
4) $\frac{15}{16}$ - $\frac{2}{7}$ = $\frac{73}{112}$
5) 274.50 ÷ 18.3 = 15
6) $\frac{2}{7}$ x 406 = 116
7) $\frac{2}{11}$ + $\frac{1}{3}$ + $\frac{3}{4}$ = $\frac{167}{132}$ or $1\frac{35}{132}$
8) 36.7 - 14.963 = 21.737

## Exercise 2.17 (page 45)
1) Division
2) Subtraction/Addition
3) Multiplication
4) Addition
5) Division

## Exercise 2.18 (page 46)
1) Multiplication
2) Subtraction/Addition
3) Addition/Multiplication
4) Addition/Division
5) Multiplication/Addition
6) Multiplication

## Exercise 2.19 (page 47)
1) Multiplication
2) Division
3) Subtraction
4) Multiplication
5) Multiplication/Addition
6) Multiplication

## Exercise 2.20 (page 48)
1) Multiplication
2) Addition/Multiplication
3) Multiplication
4) Division
5) Multiplication/Addition/Sub-traction

## Exercise 2.21 (page 49)
1) Addition
2) Multiplication
3) Addition/Division
4) Multiplication/Division
5) Subtraction
6) Addition/Division/Subtraction

## Exercise 2.22 (page 50)
1) Multiply then Divide
2) Multiply then Divide
3) Multiply then Subtract
4) Multiply or Divide then Subtract
5) Multiply then Divide
6) Multiply then Subtract

## Exercise 2.23 (page 51)
1) Add, then Add, then Divide
2) Subtract then Divide
3) Multiply then Divide
4) Multiply, then Multiply, then Divide (Answers may vary.)
5) Subtract then Divide

## Exercise 3.1 (page 53)
| 1) 13 | 2) 8 |
| 3) 28 | 4) 44 |
| 5) 2 | 6) 64 |
| 7) 10 | 8) 18 |
| 9) 3 | 10) 43 |

## Exercise 3.2 (page 54)
1) 1,460 days
2) 450 hours
3) 156 hours
4) 234 hours
5) 624 hours
6) 260 hours

## Exercise 3.3 (page 55)
| 1) $12.00 | 2) $23.79 |
| 3) $10.20 | 4) $40.96 |
| 5) $33.99 | 6) Answers will vary. |

## Exercise 3.4 (page 56)
| 1) 6.59 ft. | 2) 9 times |
| 3) 4.45 ft. | 4) 20 jumps |
| 5) 47.44 ft. | 6) 30.49 ft. |

**Exercise 3.5 (page 57)**
1) 84 cents       2) 74 cents
3) Combo B      4) $2.84
5) $\frac{1}{4}$ lb. hamburger with cheese or roast beef with nachos and large drink
6) 1 super taco with either fries or nachos and a small or medium drink

**Exercise 3.6 (page 58)**
1) 32 times      2) 6:25 a.m.
3) 6:05 p.m.     4) 9:15 a.m.
5) No

**Exercise 3.7 (page 59)**
1) 20 minutes   2) 15 minutes
3) 15 minutes   4) Friday
5) 145 minutes  6) 29 minutes
7) 42 minutes   8) 185 minutes
9) Thursday     10) 45 minutes

**Exercise 3.8 (page 60)**
1) You do NOT need to know:
 • the bakery is open five days a week.
 • the bakery is open four weeks each month.
 • how many doughnuts were sold in February and March.
2) 400 dozen doughnuts
3) 13.5 dozen
4) Charts will vary:
 January—$400.00
 February—$600.00
 March—$360.00
 April—$800.00

**Exercise 3.9 (page 61)**
1) $7\frac{1}{8}$ cups
2) 6 cups sugar
 $1\frac{1}{2}$ cups margarine
 15 T cocoa
 $1\frac{1}{2}$ cup milk
 3 T vanilla
 $11\frac{1}{4}$ cups quick oats
3) 3 cups sugar
 $\frac{3}{4}$ cup margarine
 $7\frac{1}{2}$ T cocoa
 $\frac{3}{4}$ cup milk
 $1\frac{1}{2}$ T vanilla
 $5\frac{5}{8}$ cups quick oats
4) 1 cup sugar
 $\frac{1}{4}$ cup margarine
 $2\frac{1}{2}$ T cocoa

$\frac{1}{4}$ cup milk
$\frac{1}{2}$ T vanilla
$1\frac{7}{8}$ cups quick oats

**Exercise 3.10 (page 62)**
1) $12.80       2) $31.28
3) $6.20        4) $55.88

**Exercise 3.11 (page 63)**
1) $7.35        2) $9.98
3) $42.56       4) $2.48

**Exercise 3.12 (page 64)**
1) $26.45       2) $20.00
3) $48.95       4) $31.00

**Exercise 3.13 (page 65)**
1) $52.40       2) $20.00
3) $20.00       4) $40.00
5) Yes          6) No

**Exercise 3.14 (page 66)**
1) $6.90        2) $8.10
3) $6.71 each or $20.13 total
4) $20.40

**Exercise 3.15 (page 67)**
1) $1.04        2) $5.20
3) $3.20        4) $6.32
5) $8.00

**Exercise 3.16 (page 68)**
1) $360.00
2) Between 313 and 314 boxes
3) 26 or 27 boxes
4) 43 or 44 boxes

**Exercise 3.17 (page 69)**
1) $65\frac{1}{3}$ Tablespoons
2) 1 cup
3) 3 teaspoons or 1 Tablespoon
4) $\frac{3}{4}$ cup
5) $2\frac{1}{2}$ batches

**Exercise 3.18 (page 70)**
1) 73 Tablespoons
2) 73
3) 2 cups instant tea
 3 cups sugar
 3 cups orange drink
 1 cup lemonade drink
 $3\frac{1}{2}$ teaspoons cinnamon
 $1\frac{1}{2}$ teaspoons ginger
 1 teaspoon ground cloves

4) $2\frac{1}{4}$ cups sugar
 $2\frac{1}{4}$ cups orange drink
 $\frac{3}{4}$ cup lemonade drink
 $2\frac{5}{8}$ teaspoons cinnamon
 $1\frac{1}{8}$ teaspoons ginger
 $\frac{3}{4}$ teaspoon ground cloves

**Exercise 3.19 (page 71)**
1) Stephanie:  calories = 775
        fat calories = 290
 Samantha:  calories = 1,220
        fat calories = 535
 Josie:    calories = 780
        fat calories = 335
2) Samantha, Josie, Stephanie
3) 445 calories

**Exercise 3.20 (page 72)**
1) $3.23        2) $2.62
3) about $1.50

**Exercise 3.21 (page 73)**
1) 253 calories
2) 110 calories
3) 222 calories
4) carrot and celery sticks
 grapes and celery sticks
 a peach and celery sticks
 $\frac{1}{2}$ cup strawberries and celery sticks
 a tangerine and celery sticks
 $\frac{1}{2}$ cup strawberries and carrot sticks
5) bagel and raisins
 pear and raisins
 banana and raisins

**Exercise 3.22 (page 74)**
1) $8.28        2) 9
3) 72 cents     4) Answers will vary.

**Exercise 3.23 (page 75)**
1) $25.68       2) $14.32
3) Answers will vary.

**Exercise 3.24 (page 76)**
1) $261.86
2) Yes; Possible answers are: 2 Pin Oaks, 2 Elm, 1 Pin Oak and 1 Elm, 1 Pin Oak and 1 Dogwood, or 1 Elm and 1 Dogwood.
3) More
4) Answers will vary.

## Exercise 4.1 (page 78)
1) c    2) a    3) d    4) a    5) a

## Exercise 4.2 (page 79)
1) c    2) c    3) a    4) b    5) a

## Exercise 4.3 (page 80)
1) b    2) a    3) c    4) c    5) b

## Exercise 4.4 (page 81)
1) b    2) c    3) a    4) b    5) c

## Exercise 4.5 (page 82)
1) Not reasonable; it should be around $110.00.
2) Reasonable
3) Not reasonable; it should be around $245.00.
4) Not reasonable; it should be around $117.00.
5) Reasonable

## Exercise 4.6 (page 83)
1) Reasonable
2) Reasonable
3) No; it will cost $33.70.
4) Not reasonable; the second and fourth grader should be charged $3.95 for the full buffet, which is cheaper than paying for the soup/salad bar and dessert bar separately.

## Exercise 4.7 (page 84)
1) Not reasonable; he should receive $1.75.
2) Reasonable
3) Reasonable
4) Reasonable

## Exercise 4.8 (page 85)
1) 14.83       2) 4.59
3) 22.50       4) 9.72
5) 0.27        6) 5.02
7) 38.61       8) 6.62

9) 26.8        10) 37.1
11) 7.6        12) 82.6
13) 4.5        14) 63.7
15) 10.1       16) 246.9

17) 235        18) 321
19) 37         20) 3
21) 0          22) 11
23) 50         24) 301

25) 1,500      26) 700
27) 1,000      28) 5,200
29) 8,800      30) 600

## Exercise 4.9 (page 86)
1) 132         2) 1,585
3) 11          4) 3

5) 210         6) 900
7) 8,000       8) 2,800

9) 177.0       10) 51.1
11) 2,766.3

12) 1          13) 2
14) 12         15) 15